DATE DUE			

School Desegregation and the Story of the LITTLE ROCK NINE

Mara Miller

Enslow Publishers, Inc.
40 Industrial Road
Box 398
Berkeley Heights, NJ 07922
USA

http://www.enslow.com

> *To everyone who has stood up against hatred, racism, or bigotry.*

Acknowledgments: *Special thanks to Mary Peterson*

Library of Congress Cataloging-in-Publication Data

Miller, Mara, 1968–
   School desegregation and the story of the Little Rock Nine / by Mara Miller.
     p. cm. — (From many cultures, one history)
   Includes bibliographical references.
   Audience: Grades 4–6.
   ISBN-13: 978-0-7660-2835-7
   ISBN-10: 0-7660-2835-6
     1. School integration—Arkansas—Little Rock—History—20th century—Juvenile
literature. 2. African Americans—Education—Arkansas—Little Rock—History—
20th century. 3. African American students—Arkansas—Little Rock—History—
20th century—Juvenile literature. 4. Central High School (Little Rock, Ark.)—
History—20th century—Juvenile literature. 5. Little Rock (Ark.)—Race relations—
History—20th century—Juvenile literature. I. Title.
   LC214.23.L56M56 2008
   379.2'630976773—dc22

                         2007023376
Printed in the United States of America

10 9 8 7 6 5 4 3 2 1

To Our Readers: We have done our best to make sure all Internet Addresses in this book
were active and appropriate when we went to press. However, the author and the publisher
have no control over and assume no liability for the material available on those Internet
sites or on other Web sites they may link to. Any comments or suggestions can be sent by
e-mail to comments@enslow.com or to the address on the back cover.

Every effort has been made to locate all copyright holders of material used in this book.
If any errors or omissions have occurred, corrections will be made in future editions of
this book.

Illustration Credits: Courtesy Arkansas History Commission, pp. 9, 13, 14, 39, 53, 70,
79, 85, 102, 114, 115 (right); Associated Press, pp. 4, 32, 43, 46, 75, 87, 89, 101, 107, 109,
110, 116 (right); Enslow Publishers, Inc., p. 7; Getty Images, pp. 58, 63; Library of
Congress, pp. 11, 20, 22, 26, 34, 36, 49, 66, 93, 98, 115 (left), 116 (left); Time & Life
Pictures / Getty Images, pp. 28, 60.

Cover Illustration: Courtesy Arkansas History Commission

Contents

CHAPTER 1 ☆ Facing the Crowd Alone 5

CHAPTER 2 ☆ The Path to Equal
Education 15

CHAPTER 3 ☆ "The Nine Who Dared" 31

CHAPTER 4 ☆ "The Need for Federal
Troops Is Urgent" 38

CHAPTER 5 ☆ Surviving Central High 61

CHAPTER 6 ☆ Threats From Outside
the School 76

CHAPTER 7 ☆ Ernest Graduates 81

CHAPTER 8 ☆ No School for All 88

CHAPTER 9 ☆ How Far We've Come 99

Where Are They Now? 111

Timeline 114

Chapter Notes 117

Glossary 123

Further Reading and
Internet Addresses 125

Index 126

Thousands of people on the front lawn of Central High School in Little Rock, Arkansas, in 1997 celebrate the fortieth anniversary of the integration of the school. In 1957, a hateful crowd confronted the nine black students that wanted to attend classes within its walls.

CHAPTER One

Facing the Crowd Alone

It was 1957. Central High School sat like a forbidden castle—forbidden to people of color, like the white-only restrooms, diners, and railcars that were common in Little Rock, Arkansas, and other southern states at the time. But things were changing. Three years earlier, the United States Supreme Court decided that segregation in schools based on race was unconstitutional. *Segregation* means "separation." The U.S. Supreme Court is the highest court in the United States. This 1954 decision meant keeping black students out of schools attended by whites was illegal. For the first time in history, black students would walk through Central High School's stone and marble halls to attend classes.

Many people were unhappy with the Supreme Court's decision. In the 1950s, racism was widespread. This was especially true in southern states where enslaved Africans had once been used for labor. Racism is a belief that certain people are inferior based on physical features such as skin or hair color. Racist groups such as the Ku Klux Klan (KKK) used their belief in white supremacy to justify horrible crimes, including murder.

Most black families celebrated the Court's decision. But many were nervous. They worried that the desegregation would result in revenge from white people. They were afraid that they would lose their jobs. Or worse, they were afraid of mob violence against black people. They had reason to be afraid. Lynching happened too often in the Deep South. Lynching is killing somebody accused of a crime without a fair trial. Usually the victim is hung from a tree. Most lynching happened to black men.

In spite of their families' concerns, some black students spent the summer preparing to attend Central High that fall. It's not easy to enter a new school. And the students knew that starting this new school would be even more difficult. They attended numerous meetings and interviews. They were told how to behave and what to expect. School officials actually tried to discourage the students from making the transfer. Despite their fears, the students were excited.

ARKANSAS

MISSOURI

Fort Smith

TENN.

LITTLE ROCK ⭐

OKLA.

Hot Springs

MISSISSIPPI

TEXAS

LOUISIANA

Little Rock is the capital of Arkansas and was considered by many to be a good place to begin integration. However, Governor Orval Faubus, backed by a group of segregationists, turned the integration into a national crisis.

Elizabeth Eckford Faces the Mob Alone

Elizabeth Eckford, one of the black students, pressed the black and white skirt she had sewn for the first day of school. The television blared in the background. Elizabeth's mother told her to turn it off. She was too worried to listen to anymore news. Two nights before, the governor of Arkansas had called out the National Guard. He had said they were there to keep the peace, but few people knew what their orders actually were. People wondered if they would protect the black students or keep them from entering the school. Elizabeth's dad paced with a sad and nervous expression. But Elizabeth was confident. She boarded a city bus and rode to Central High.

When Elizabeth got off the bus, she encountered a mob of people. She had not heard about a plan for the new black students to meet at the corner of Twelfth and Park streets. Instead she headed for the front of the school. She was nervous but not afraid. She was certain the guardsmen would protect her if the crowd got out of control.

At one point, she tried to pass a line of soldiers to get into the school. They would not let her through. Then one of the guards pointed across the street. Elizabeth thought he meant she should cross the street and go to the main entrance. She crossed and continued to walk.

Elizabeth Eckford speaks with a National Guardsman as he points across the street.

The crowd followed behind her. The people moved like a single organism. They began shouting and calling Elizabeth names. They yelled, "Go home before you get hurt nigger" and "Why don't you go back to the god-damn jungle!"[1]

Elizabeth kept her head held high and walked until she was standing in front of the main door. She looked at the school surrounded by the National

Guard. It was very big. The main building was more than two blocks long and contained one hundred classrooms. Statues of Greek goddesses decorated the entry. The campus was four square blocks.

Summoning courage, Elizabeth tried to follow a white student inside. The soldiers closed ranks. They would not let her through. When she tried to squeeze past again, the soldiers raised their bayonets. The guardsmen were not there to protect the students or stop any violence. They were there to stop the black students from entering the school.

Elizabeth started to panic. Fear rose as the crowd moved closer. Someone shouted: "Lynch her!"[2] Elizabeth held her books and looked for a friendly face. When she thought she found one, the woman spat on her. She saw a bus stop a block away and began walking toward it. The crowd was at her heels shouting insults. Someone yelled, "Get a rope and drag her over to this tree."[3]

Keeping her eyes forward, Elizabeth made it to the bus stop's bench. A *New York Times* reporter sat next to her and put his arm around her. Tears were streaming from under her dark glasses. The reporter lifted her chin, "Don't let them see you cry," he told her.[4] Grace Lorch, a white professor's wife, sat on the other side of her.

Lorch yelled at the mob, "Leave this child alone. . . . Six months from now, you will hang your heads in shame."[5] Members of the crowd yelled insults at

African-American student Elizabeth Eckford studies at home after being turned away from Central High School.

Lorch and told her to leave. They did not want her to protect Elizabeth. When Lorch tried to call a cab for Elizabeth, members of the crowd blocked Lorch's access to a phone.

Fortunately, the bus came. Lorch boarded with Elizabeth and sat next to her. She tried to talk to Elizabeth, but the girl was too shaken to answer. Elizabeth rode to where her mother worked at a school for the blind. She ran inside and up the stairs. When Elizabeth saw the fear in her mother's expression, all she could do was hug her mother and cry.

A Second Escape

Melba Pattillo, another one of the new black students, drove with her mother to the school. They parked several blocks away from the arranged meeting place. The mob made it impossible for them to get any closer. As Melba and her mother walked, they looked for friendly faces but did not see any. Then they saw Elizabeth trying to enter the school. They watched as the guardsmen repeatedly blocked her entrance. Melba wanted to help Elizabeth but could not push her way through the crowd. She and her mother prayed for Elizabeth's safety as the crowd began to chant "Get her, Get the nigger out of there."[6]

The crowd was becoming more aggressive. Melba and her mother sensed that they were in a dangerous situation. They tried to turn around and quietly walk back to their car. But two white men noticed and

Police use a barricade to keep the crowd back on the first day that nine black students tried to attend Central High School in Little Rock, Arkansas.

started to chase them. Another white man joined in, carrying a rope. The men were violent and angry. Melba got the car keys from her mother. Melba's mother told her to leave without her if she had to. Melba was able to get both her mother and herself in the car before gunning it in reverse to make an escape.

On Governor Faubus's Orders

The other black students were jostled and shoved as they made their way toward the school. For safety's sake, they walked between four ministers—two white and two black. The crowd jeered. Reporters

A National Guardsman prevents African-American students from entering Central High School on September 4, 1957. From the left are Carlotta Walls, Gloria Ray, Jane Hill, and Ernest Green. After September 4, Hill decided not to attend.

asked the students questions, and photographers snapped their pictures.

When the students reached the school, it was the same as it had been with Elizabeth. The guardsmen would not let them enter. One of the ministers asked a captain of the guardsmen why. The officer answered that they were acting on orders from Governor Orval Faubus.

CHAPTER Two

The Path to Equal Education

Education has long been regarded as a pathway to power. So much so that when slaves were used as forced labor in the southern states, it was illegal in almost all slave states to teach a slave to read or write. Slave owners were afraid that if slaves learned these skills, they would forge traveling documents and escape to freedom.

After the Civil War ended in 1865, Congress passed the Thirteenth Amendment, which abolished (ended) slavery in the United States. Congress then passed two amendments, or additions, to the Constitution to protect the rights of African Americans. The Fourteenth Amendment (1868) guaranteed citizenship and equal protection under the law to anyone born or naturalized in the United States. This was very important to the newly freed slaves who would now be U.S. citizens. This amendment prevented states from making or enforcing laws that reduced the privileges or protections granted to citizens. No state could take away life, liberty, or property without due process of law. And all citizens were granted equal protection under the law. The Fifteenth Amendment (1870) granted black men the right to vote. This amendment says that the right to vote "cannot be denied or abridged by race, color, or previous condition of servitude." (white and black women would not get to vote until 1920.)

Congress also created a Freedman's Bureau to help the newly freed slaves. Most former slaves had little education and no money or property. One of the bureau's responsibilities and its biggest success was education.

New Schools for New Citizens

The newly freed slaves knew the importance of education to equality. One Freedman's Bureau agent reported in 1865 that when he told three thousand newly freed slaves they would be educated, "They fairly jumped and shouted in gladness."[1]

Missionaries taught children by day and adults by night. "I never before saw children so eager to learn," said Charlotte Forten. She was the daughter of the wealthy African-American shipyard owner James Forten. She taught on an island off the coast of South Carolina. "Coming to school is a constant delight and recreation to them," she wrote. "They come here as other children go to play. The older ones, during the summer, work in the fields from early morning until eleven or twelve o'clock, and then come into school, after their hard toil in the hot sun, as bright and anxious to learn as ever."[2] A newly freed slave said he would make sure his children went to school because he considered "education [the] next best thing to liberty."[3]

Schools opened wherever there was space—sometimes in tents, shanties, barns, and even outside at open meetings. As more schools opened, both black and white students began taking advantage of the free educational opportunities. Over time, a public school system developed in the South.

Steps Backward

Many white southerners felt that the three amendments protecting the newly freed slaves were forced on their states after the Civil War. Many were still angry that slavery had been abolished. As time passed, the northern states grew less interested in the rights of African-American citizens and more interested in the growing economy. The rights granted and protected by the Fourteenth and Fifteenth amendments were chipped away in the South by state and local laws.

These laws, known as "Jim Crow laws," were enacted in many southern states. Jim Crow was a theater character made up by a white man to make fun of blacks. Jim Crow laws were designed to keep African Americans from gaining true equality. Blacks and whites were separated by race in railroad cars, schools, restaurants, parks, theaters, churches, and even in bathrooms and at drinking fountains. The best facilities were saved for white people.

Many southern states effectively took away African Americans' right to vote. The Fifteenth Amendment says no state can prohibit voting by race. So the white politicians used property owner- ship, literacy tests, and poll taxes as a requirement for voting. Most slaves had not been educated and very few owned property or had the money to pay the tax on voting. When African Americans did meet the requirements, state voting officials often made the questions they asked impossible to answer. One question that a voting official in the South asked an African-American man was: "How many bubbles are there in a cake of soap?" When the man did not have an answer, he was told to go home.[4]

Plessy's Challenge

In the 1890s, Homer Plessy challenged these laws. Plessy, a black man, entered a railcar marked whites- only. When he refused to leave, he was arrested. He sued the state of Louisiana, asserting that the separation marked him as inferior. At issue was the meaning of the Fourteenth Amendment.

His case went to the U.S. Supreme Court. In 1896, the Court handed down the majority decision. It stated that while the Fourteenth Amendment's objective had been to enforce equality between the two races before the law, "it could not have been intended to abolish distinctions based upon color, or to enforce social, as distinguished from political equality, or a commingling of the two races upon terms unsatisfactory to either."[5] They had ruled that segregation was legal.

Only one associate justice disagreed. Justice John Marshall Harlan foresaw the terrible consequences. He said that "our Constitution is color-blind" and that "the interests of both [races] require that the common government of all shall not permit the seeds of race hate to be planted under the sanction of law."[6] But he was only one of nine justices.

Separate Is Not Equal

Throughout the South, the separate facilities were rarely, if ever, equal. The drinking fountains marked for blacks did not work as well and were sometimes dirty, while the better water fountains would say whites-only. African Americans were forced to sit in the backs of buses. Many stores and restaurants were off-limits to them as well. Those that were open to black customers would serve all their white customers first, and some would only serve black customers out the back door. Whites-only waiting

An African-American man drinks from a "Colored Only" water cooler in a streetcar terminal in Oklahoma City, Oklahoma.

rooms in railway stations would be bigger and have more seats. Sometimes the waiting rooms for African Americans would not even have heat.

White citizens often became enraged when these unfair rules were broken. Melba Pattillo, one of the black students who tried to attend Central High, remembers being an eight-year-old and having to go to the bathroom. The bathroom for white people was much closer. (They were usually closer. There were more whites-only bathrooms, and they were in central locations.) Her curiosity combined with the urgent need sent her running into the forbidden restroom.

She barely had time to notice how much nicer, bigger, and cleaner the whites-only bathroom was compared to those she usually used. But she did notice. It was as pretty as she had imagined. The women inside the bathroom screamed at her and called her "nigger." They ordered her to get out. But it was too late. She had already sat down to go to the bathroom. When she finished, the police were waiting for her outside the bathroom door. Her grandmother spent over an hour explaining to the police before they would let them go.

Undoing the Plessy Decision

During World War II (1939–1945), both black and white soldiers risked their lives and fought for freedom. Although the black soldiers had fought as hard and risked as much as their white counterparts, they were not considered equal. They had witnessed the evils of racism overseas in Adolf Hitler's regime, only to find them again at home. This made a lot of the black veterans angry. They had risked their lives for freedom in Europe. They were willing to risk them again for equality in the United States.

It had been nearly fifty years since the U.S. Supreme Court's *Plessy* v. *Ferguson* decision. The idea of "separate, but equal" was firmly set in the laws

African-American soldiers train during World War II.

of the southern states and the minds of many. Only the U.S. Supreme Court could overturn the *Plessy* v. *Ferguson* decision. The Supreme Court changing one of its previous decisions is rare. But it was a different time and there were nine different justices on the Court.

The NAACP and Charles Huston's Plan

World War II had unsettled many white Americans as well. They also saw the racism that they hated in Germany reflected at home. In 1948, President Truman desegregated the military. The time was ripe for change and the National Association for the Advancement of Colored People (NAACP) had a plan.

The NAACP is an organization that fights to end racial discrimination. It began in response to a race riot in Springfield, Illinois. During the riot, eight African-American men died. Two thousand more African Americans left the city out of fear for their lives. Afterward, fifty-three mostly white social workers, educators, lawyers, and clergy members signed a letter attacking racism and defending the rights of black Americans. A year later, many of the signers joined and formed the organization.

In 1934, the NAACP hired Charles Hamilton Huston as full-time legal counsel. Huston had been a law professor at Howard University in Washington D.C. There, he taught his students to be the best attorneys they could be. He believed that the law was a powerful weapon that could help the disadvantaged. He carefully studied the rules of law and the court opinions of prior cases. Then he developed a legal plan for the NAACP. Instead of challenging the idea of having separate facilities, Huston would attack the unequal nature of them.

It was easy to prove that schools and other African-American facilities were inferior. Schools for African-American children were usually overcrowded. The buildings were often in poor condition and many did not have indoor plumbing. Black students were often bussed considerable distances although a white school might be much closer. The all-black schools were often poorly equipped. Students might not have desks and the books were often the old and discarded copies from white schools. Author and historian, Richard Kluger, described one all-black junior high school's science lab as consisting of "a Bunsen burner and a bowl of goldfish."[7]

Huston hoped that if states had to provide truly equal facilities, the cost would be too high and the states would be forced to end segregation. He also hoped that by getting lower court rulings in the NAACP's favor, they would be able to prove that separate could never be equal.

Thurgood Marshall Joins the Fight

At Howard University, Charles Huston taught a young attorney named Thurgood Marshall. Marshall was a star debater and Huston's best student. When Huston accepted the NAACP's job offer, he asked them to hire Marshall as well.

Huston and Marshall made an amazing legal team. One of their first victories was for Donald Murray. Murray was a black student who wanted to attend the University of Maryland's law school. Huston and Marshall argued that Murray could not get an equal education at Princess Anne Academy, the alternative school open to black students. Princess Anne Academy did not even have a law degree available. The court ruled in favor of Murray.

The University of Maryland was forced to change its policies on race.

In 1938, Marshall took the reins from his mentor and became chief counsel of the NAACP's legal defense and education fund. During the next twelve years, he fought many legal battles. He was a talented attorney and won many cases including several that ended segregation in higher education. But Marshall had bigger goals. He wanted to "obtain full and complete integration of all students on all levels of public education without regard to race or color."[8]

In 1950, several court cases in the South challenged segregation in elementary schools. Marshall and other NAACP attorneys argued these cases in the lower courts of South Carolina, Kansas, Delaware, Virginia, and Washington, D.C. The cases were appealed until they reached the U.S. Supreme Court. There they were combined into one case. The names of the thirteen plaintiffs (the parents of the twenty children involved in the suit) were written alphabetically. The case name was too long and therefore shortened to *Brown* (the first name on the list) v. *Board of Education*. In December of 1952, the Supreme Court heard the first oral (spoken) arguments.

Brown v. *Board of Education*

Marshall worried about the outcome of the *Brown* v. *Board of Education* case. People had risked time,

Thurgood Marshall

As chief counsel for the NAACP, Thurgood Marshall was one of the most important civil rights activists of his time.

Marshall grew up in segregated Baltimore. His principal punished him by making him memorize parts of the U.S. Constitution. By graduation, he knew the whole document by heart. He knew that some of the words he memorized did not fit with the racism and segregation he faced.

Thurgood's father, William Marshall, never told Thurgood to become a lawyer. But he turned him into one. "He did it by teaching me to argue, by challenging my logic on every point, by making me prove every statement I made," Marshall later recalled.[9]

During his time with the NAACP, beginning in 1936, Marshall won twenty-seven out of thirty-two cases that went to the Supreme Court. In 1967, President Lyndon B. Johnson nominated Marshall for the U.S. Supreme Court. Marshall, the Court's first African-American justice, served until 1991.

Thurgood Marshall died on January 24, 1993.

money, security, and their very safety. People who were involved were often fired from their jobs, and sometimes their lives were threatened. Marshall knew he needed to move forward. But he worried that the families' sacrifice would be for nothing.

In court, Marshall argued that separate schools resulted in feelings of inferiority. He used new psychological evidence to show that black children were harmed by racial discrimination. Psychologist Kenneth Clark tested children's attitudes using dolls of different races. He found that black children when asked which dolls were prettier or nicer would generally point to the white dolls, indicating that the black dolls were less pretty or less nice. This showed that black children saw themselves as inferior to whites. It was evidence that discrimination was harming these children's ideas about themselves.

In oral arguments, Marshall challenged the idea that black and white children would have problems if schools were desegregated. "Everyone knows that is not true," he told the Court. "Those same kids in Virginia and South Carolina . . . they play in the streets together, they play on their farms together, they go down the road together, they separate to go to school, they come out of school and play ball together."[10]

Later in written arguments, Marshall argued that the only way that racial restrictions could be considered constitutional would be if the Court ruled

Above are children who were involved in the Brown v. Board of Education *case. From the left are: Vicki Henderson, Donald Henderson, Linda Brown (after whom the case was named), James Emanuel, Nancy Todd, and Katherine Carper.*

that African Americans were inferior and therefore should be separated from other human beings. This put additional pressure on the Court to go beyond the historical and legal arguments and determine what was ethical or the right thing to do. With Marshall's powerful speeches, brilliant legal arguments, and flawless presentation (he would rather retype his work than let it have a typo), it was hard for anyone to say he was inferior.

Chief Justice Earl Warren

Although the individual school-discrimination cases began in 1950 and reached the Supreme Court in December 1952, it was not until 1954 that a decision was announced. In September 1953, Chief Justice Fred M. Vinson died. President Dwight D. Eisenhower appointed former California Governor Earl Warren to take his place. Vinson believed in segregation. Justice Warren was against it.

When Warren took office, there were probably enough votes to overturn the *Plessy* v. *Ferguson* decision on a 5 to 4 vote. But Warren felt the Court needed to speak with one voice. He took every opportunity he had to talk to the four members who disagreed. By March, the votes were 8 to 1 to overturn. By May, it was unanimous.

On May 17, 1954, Warren read the decision:

> To separate [children] from others of similar age and qualifications solely because of their race generates a feeling of inferiority as to their status in their

community that may affect their hearts and minds in a way unlikely to ever be undone. . . . [Therefore,] we conclude that in the field of public education the doctrine of "separate but equal" has no place.[11]

"With All Deliberate Speed"

For Marshall, the only disappointment with the *Brown* v. *Board of Education* decision was that it had not set a date for integration. It took almost another year before the Court stated how the decision should be applied. This decision further disappointed Marshall. The decree stated that desegregation should take place "with all deliberate speed." The Court wanted to give schools time to prepare. But Marshall knew that the Court's language would give southern states time to delay.

In Little Rock, the school district announced that it would comply within five days of the decision. School superintendent Virgil Blossom proposed a plan for gradual desegregation starting at the high school level. All-black schools would remain, but a small number of chosen students would be allowed into the all-white Central High School starting in 1957. Integration would then gradually move to the elementary schools in the following years until anyone who wished to transfer could.

Black families saw the "Blossom plan" as a way of stalling. The NAACP challenged the plan in court because it was too slow. But the court decided that the plan met the requirement of all deliberate speed.

CHAPTER Three

"The Nine Who Dared"

The year before integration, teachers in Little Rock's all-black schools asked their students if any of them were interested in transferring to Central High School the following fall. About 70 to 80 students expressed an interest.[1] Most of these students were screened out. The school officials said they were picking only the best and brightest students to help make integration a success. But some observers felt the purpose of the process was to talk the black students out of transferring.

Only seventeen students remained after the screening. Seven of them withdrew before school began. Another, Jane Hill, returned to the all-black Horace Mann High School after being turned away from Central High on September 4. In all, nine students attended Central High. These nine students

Gloria Ray

Terrence Roberts

Melba Pattillo

Minnijean Brown

Ernest Green

Elizabeth Eckford

Jefferson Thomas

Carlotta Walls

Thelma Mothershed

THE LITTLE ROCK NINE

The nine African Americans above braved angry crowds to become the first black students at Central High School. They are known as the Little Rock Nine.

were on the battle lines of desegregation. Their intense experiences made them a sort of family. They became known as the Little Rock Nine.

The Little Rock Nine

Ernest Green was the oldest. He started Central High as a senior. His eyes were warm and he had an easy smile. His father's death in World War II made him grow up early. Smart and well-spoken, he told his mother that he wanted to attend Central High. He felt that the *Brown* decision opened a window of opportunity for him to be a part of African American history. He already knew that "if things were going to change, it wasn't going to be handed to [him]."[2] His mother pointed out the difficulty of entering a new school in his senior year. However, she said she would stand behind him.

Elizabeth Eckford was also determined to go to Central High. Her mother tried to delay registering her. She hoped Elizabeth would forget about it. But Elizabeth did not. After two weeks passed, she told her mother, "We're going to the school board office [to register] and we're going today."[3] Elizabeth was only fifteen years old and very shy by nature. But she wanted to be a lawyer. She thought attending Central High would help her become one.[4]

Melba Pattillo would enter Central High as a junior. She raised her hand on a whim when her teacher asked for students who wanted to transfer.

The Little Rock Nine pose with Daisy Bates (second from right, back row), in her living room.

She never discussed her interest with her family. They were surprised when they learned that she was assigned to Central High. Her father demanded that she not attend. His boss was threatening to fire him if she did. Her grandmother, however, rose to the occasion. She told her son that African-American people getting a quality education was more important than his job.[5] Her Auntie Mae said that Melba "was just sassy enough to pull [integration] off."[6]

Minnijean Brown was a good friend of Melba's. They lived a block apart. Both loved to sing, and both were tall for their age. Minnijean's father wanted her to attend Central, but her mother was afraid for her safety. Minnijean was outgoing, friendly, and wanted to fit in. She had no problem expressing her emotions. Her temper, reasonable but quicker than the others, made her a target during the school year.

Jefferson Thomas would enter Central High as a sophomore. He had the type of subtle humor that made people laugh when they were not supposed to. Slim and athletic, he was a track star at his old school. He was also the student-council president. He was willing to give those things up for the opportunities he felt that Central High School offered. Jefferson wanted to go to college and had dreams of being great someday. Most of the black schools did not have college preparatory classes for his chosen interests.[7]

Thelma Mothershed was another determined student. At age sixteen, she was small and often pale due to a heart condition. Her parents worried that transferring to Central High would hurt her heart. They called a family meeting. Her two sisters, both in college, came home to discuss it. One of her sisters was the first African American to attend Enid University in Oklahoma. At the end of the family meeting, Thelma got her wish. She registered for Central High. The stress would prove hard on

Jefferson Thomas (left) and Ernest Green read about their efforts to attend Central High in a newspaper.

her heart. It would cause her to collapse during her first day in the school. But in spite of her heart condition, she would have near perfect attendance for the year.

Gloria Ray's father also had a heart condition. Gloria's mother was so worried about her husband's heart that she did not tell him about Gloria's transfer to Central High. He learned of it on the television the first day of school. He then offered to send Gloria to any private school of her choice. She told her dad that she loved him dearly and certainly would not do anything to impair his health. But quit Central High? No. That was something she could not do.

Terrence Roberts was fifteen and searching for a place where things were different. Like the others, he could not understand the hatred shown to him by white people he did not even know. When the school board came and asked who would be willing to enroll in Central High, Terrence raised his hand. He hoped that it would be the start of a positive change. He hoped that he would not have to leave Arkansas to find a place where he was not judged by the color of his skin. His parents supported his decision. With a pencil tucked behind his ear, he often hummed a cheerful tune. His funny and intelligent commentary would make his fellow students smile.

Carlotta Walls declared that she would attend Central High even if she had to go it alone.[8] She liked to swim, bowl, and play baseball. Rosa Parks, a civil rights leader who had refused to give up her seat on an Alabama bus to a white person, inspired Carlotta to get the best education she could. So, when her homeroom teacher passed around a paper for students to sign if they were interested in attending Central High, she wrote her name. Her parents supported her decision, but her young mother's hair turned almost white with worry during that first year.[9]

CHAPTER Four

"The Need for Federal Troops Is Urgent"

A few weeks before school started, Daisy Bates was listening to the news in her living room. A rock shattered her window. The rock came with a note that read: "Stone this time. Dynamite Next."[1]

Daisy Bates was the president of the Arkansas branch of the NAACP. Bates was very involved in the planned desegregation. She and her husband, L. C. Bates, also ran a small newspaper.

Their paper, the *Arkansas State Press*, spoke out against violence and discrimination. They reported and condemned police brutality against black citizens. They took up the cause of black World War II veterans who came home to harassment and racism after fighting for their country. Reporting these

Daisy Bates

Daisy Gatson was seven years old when she first encountered the evils of racism. Her mother sent her to the store for pork chops. The butcher told her that "niggers have to wait 'til I wait on the white people."[2]

Daisy Bates and her husband, L. C. Bates (front right)

A year later, Daisy's mother was murdered while resisting rape by three white men. Daisy was filled with anger and hate. But she loved and admired her adoptive parents.

Daisy Gatson would grow up to become an integral part of the civil rights movement. She married a journalist named Lucious Christopher, also known as L.C., Bates. Together they published a newspaper that spoke out against the mistreatment of African Americans.

In 1952, Daisy Bates became the leader of the Arkansas branch of the NAACP. She continued working for the NAACP until 1972.

In 1962, she wrote a book about the Little Rock crisis called *The Long Shadow of Little Rock*. It was republished in 1986 and won the American Book Award.

Eighty-five-year-old Daisy Bates died in 1999.

truths sometimes resulted in advertisers pulling their money from the paper. Advertising is the life blood of a newspaper, and the *Arkansas State Press* was often low on funds. But Daisy and L. C. Bates stuck to their beliefs and the paper survived.

Threats and Delays

Throughout the summer, segregationists worked to stop integration from happening. A group called the Capital Citizen's Council purchased ads that encouraged people to "write, wire, or phone" Governor Faubus and tell him to stop the "race-mixing."[3] They hosted a dinner for three hundred segregationists, featuring Governor Marvin Griffin of Georgia. Speaking to the crowd, Griffin urged them to join his state in resisting integration. The crowd clapped and cheered.

Segregationists also tried to challenge the decision in court. On August 29, they asked Judge Murray O. Reed for an order to stop integration. Governor Faubus testified about a rumor that the white and black youths were forming gangs. He said he personally knew that "revolvers had been taken from Negro and white pupils." Judge Reed granted the injunction. Reporters investigated Governor Faubus's claim but did not find any evidence to verify it.[4]

That night, the segregationists celebrated. They drove around town blaring their horns, and yelling, "The Coons Won't Be Going to Central."[5] The NAACP filed a petition with Federal Judge Ronald N. Davies the next day. Judge Davies overrode Judge Reed's decision and ordered the school board to continue with integration.

Then on Labor Day weekend, as most of the Little Rock Nine were enjoying their last night before school with picnics and swimming, Governor Faubus prepared to address the state. Jefferson Thomas was visiting Daisy Bates at the time. Together, they wondered what Faubus would say.

"Is there anything they can do—now that they lost in court? Is there anyway they can stop us from entering Central tomorrow morning?" Jefferson asked Bates.[6]

Bates did not think so. But at around 7:00 P.M., a newspaper reporter came to her door. He asked if she knew that the National Guard was surrounding the school. She did not. She and her husband quickly drove to Central High to see what was happening.

Army trucks and jeeps lined the street. Soldiers wearing helmets and carrying guns with bayonets were piling out of trucks and climbing the stairs in front of the school. It was almost too much to believe.

Daisy Bates rushed home to hear Governor Faubus's speech.

Orval Faubus Stirs Up Trouble

Governor Orval Faubus was tall and hawkish. His dark, thinning hair was slicked back in the style of the time. He wore a dark suit and dark tie. He had a way of making people feel that he was one of them. He announced that knives and weapons were being purchased in alarming numbers. He said that caravans of white supremacists were coming to Little Rock. He predicted that "blood [would] run in the streets" if the African-American students attempted to start school the next day.[7]

> I must state here in all sincerity, that it is my opinion, yes, even a conviction, that it will not be possible to restore or to maintain order and protect the lives and property of the citizens if forcible integration is carried out tomorrow in the schools of this community. . . . therefore . . . the schools in Pulaski County, for the time being, must be operated on the same basis as they have been operated in the past.[8]

In his speech, the governor had forbidden the nine students from entering Central High.

There is little evidence that there was a significant threat or that caravans of people were coming to the school before Faubus's interference. But his speech caused uproar and panic in both the black and white communities. As Melba Pattillo's grandmother said, "[Faubus] was stirring up trouble by talking about trouble."[9]

Faubus's speech gave many segregationists more confidence. They had reason to believe that the governor was on their side. Phones started ringing all around Little Rock. Some of the callers threatened the black students. One caller told Melba Pattillo that he knew her address and would be over to bomb the house. Another said, "Niggers don't belong in our schools. You-all are made for hanging."[10]

Melba's grandmother sat up all night with a shotgun. Melba wrote in her diary: "Maybe going to Central High isn't such a good idea after all. It's costing my family a lot of agony and energy. Will grandma always have to sit up guarding us?"[11]

Arkansas Governor Orval Faubus sits at his desk in the governor's mansion in Little Rock in September 1957.

What Did Faubus's Speech Mean?

The parents of the Little Rock Nine contacted Daisy Bates. They wanted to know what the speech meant. They feared for their children's safety. The governor had said that "blood would run in the streets."[12]

Elizabeth Eckford's mother, Birdie, told Daisy Bates about seeing a lynch mob when she was a girl in 1927. She witnessed the mob dragging a black man down the street. The mob had later used church pews to burn the man's body. Bates tried to reassure Mrs. Eckford. There had been a lot of progress in Little Rock since 1927. Governor Faubus had said in his speech that the troops were there for protection.

He had assured the people that the guardsmen were neither segregationist nor integrationist. They were soldiers with assigned tasks. The troops would protect the students, she reasoned.

The NAACP lawyers went back to Judge Ronald Davies, who was in charge of the Arkansas desegregation cases. The lawyers wanted to find out what they should do about the delay and the governor's statement. Judge Davies said that he was taking the governor at "face value."[13] The troops were there to protect citizens and property. He did not think they were there to stop desegregation. He told the NAACP and school officials that the students should start school the next morning.

The school superintendent Virgil Blossom spoke to the nine students and their parents. He asked that adults not be present the next day when the students came to school. He said it would be easier to protect them if they came alone.

Sending Those Kids Alone Would Be Murder

The idea of sending the students alone made Daisy Bates and some of the parents uneasy. Then a young reporter came to Daisy Bates's door. Sending those kids alone would be "murder," he told her. The crowd was growing and "they've gone mad."[14] Daisy Bates knew she had to keep the kids safe. She asked church ministers to walk with the children the next day.

Surely the mob would not attack leaders of a church. The minister she spoke with said he would be there. But he did not know how many others would come.

Daisy Bates also called the police. She told an officer her concerns and what she had heard about the crowd. The officer promised to have a squad car near the school. But he would not be able to help after the students neared the school grounds. The police were forbidden to get close to the school as long as the troops were there.

Finally, Bates called the families. It was after 2:00 A.M. She told the students to meet at Twelfth and Park streets at 8:30 A.M., so they could walk with the church ministers. Bates was unable to speak with Elizabeth Eckford's family. The Eckfords did not have a phone in their home. By 3:00 A.M., Bates decided it would be best to tell Elizabeth in the morning. Exhausted, she went to sleep.

The next morning, Daisy and L. C. Bates drove to the meeting place. As they drove, they heard on the car radio that an African-American student was being mobbed in front of the school. Daisy Bates felt sick. It had to be Elizabeth. In the morning rush, Bates had forgotten to tell her about the plan to meet and walk as a group. Daisy Bates prayed for Elizabeth's safety as L.C. rushed to find her. She was relieved when L.C. came back and said that Elizabeth had safely boarded a bus. She was also thankful to see four ministers, two white and two

As the Little Rock Nine were trying to integrate Central High School, six African-American students, with the help of ministers, tried to integrate a high school in the town of North Little Rock, Arkansas. The students and ministers did not have the support of the school board. Above, white students deny access to the black students.

black, waiting and willing to walk with the rest of the students.

Racial Tension Increases

After the students were turned away, racial tension increased in Little Rock. The crowd around the school grew. The FBI investigated the governor's reports of potential violence. The U.S. Attorney General Herbert Brownell asked for an injunction against the governor. This would be a legal order forcing the governor to stop interfering. A court date was set for September 20.

Until the court date, the Little Rock Nine had little choice but to wait. Most of them were confined to their homes. Their parents feared they would be attacked if seen outside. Their phones rang with threats. Melba's house was shot at. Her grandmother returned fire and scared the gunmen away.

The nine students tried to keep up with their schoolwork. Teachers at Central High sent them their assignments. Grace Lorch, the woman who had sat with Elizabeth on the bus bench, organized tutoring sessions. She and her husband held classes for the students at the local community college.

Governor Faubus Meets With President Eisenhower

Governor Faubus asked to see President Dwight D. Eisenhower. The president agreed to meet with Faubus. Eisenhower had not shown support for the *Brown* v. *Board of Education* decision. He did not believe laws should be forced on people from the top down. He was concerned that the Supreme Court had overstepped its bounds. He had even said that he could not imagine a situation that would cause him to send federal troops to enforce orders of a federal court. President Eisenhower's stance on the issue encouraged the segregationists. Many black leaders worried what the president and governor would decide behind closed doors without anyone representing African Americans.

However, Eisenhower was a man of duty. He told a friend in a letter the summer before the crisis that:

> there must be respect for the Constitution—which means the Supreme Court's interpretation of the Constitution—or we shall have chaos. We cannot possibly imagine a successful form of government in which every individual citizen would have the right to interpret the Constitution according to his own convictions, beliefs, and prejudices.[15]

When the two men met, Eisenhower did not suggest that Governor Faubus remove the troops. Rather, he encouraged him to change their orders. Faubus could direct the troops "to preserve order, but to allow the Negro children to attend Central High School."[16] Eisenhower also told Faubus that he did not want to see any governor humiliated. But if it came to a confrontation between federal and state governments, "the state would lose."[17]

Governor Faubus returned to Arkansas. But he did not remove the troops or change their orders.

The Injunction Against Governor Faubus

Thurgood Marshall, Daisy Bates, and the nine students went to court on Friday, September 20, for

President Dwight Eisenhower (left) and Arkansas Governor Orval Faubus leave a meeting at the "summer White House" in Newport, Rhode Island, on September 14, 1957.

Eisenhower and Civil Rights

President Eisenhower was moderate on civil rights. As a general, he initially opposed the desegregation of the Army. He also had many white friends and supporters in the South who were in favor of segregation. Sometimes he seemed uncomfortable with African-American leaders.

However, Eisenhower was generally against discrimination. In high school, he defended an African-American athlete who was harassed and kicked off a school team by the coach. Later, he refused to stay in a hotel because it said that African Americans and Jews were not welcome. As president, he continued the desegregation of the Army and even desegregated the Army schools before the Supreme Court's *Brown* v. *Board of Education* decision. He was also the first president to hire an African American for an executive position.

In a letter responding to famed African-American baseball player, Jackie Robinson, Eisenhower said that he was "firmly on record as believing that every citizen of every race and creed deserves to enjoy equal civil rights and liberties."[18]

But it was not the race issue that brought Eisenhower into the Little Rock conflict. Eisenhower saw danger in allowing a state to override a federal mandate.

the hearing against the governor. Melba Pattillo hoped to meet Governor Faubus. She wanted him to see that there was "nothing so bad about [her] that he shouldn't allow white children to go to school with [her]."[19] But Governor Faubus did not show up at the hearing. His attorneys came alone. They made several motions to postpone the case. They even asked the judge to disqualify himself from presiding (being in charge) over the case. Judge Davies refused these motions and Faubus's attorneys left.

Thurgood Marshall was astounded. He had never seen anything like that in court. Judge Davies ordered that the hearing continue. He listened to Mayor Woodrow Wilson Mann, school officials, Police Chief Marvin Potts, and some of the nine students. They testified that there had not been significant threats to warrant the calling of the National Guard. Judge Davies ruled that Governor Faubus, by the use of the National Guard had, "thwarted" the court-approved plan for integration. He forbade the governor from further interference. Faubus had to remove the troops. The Little Rock Nine would start school on Monday.

Hate Erupts

Judge Davies's decision was not welcome news to the growing crowd surrounding the school. By Monday, the mob raged and grew restless waiting for the African-American students to arrive. The National

Guard was gone. A much smaller number of police was assigned to control the mob and protect the nine students.

The students met at Daisy Bates's home. They divided into two cars. For the students' safety, the drivers would take indirect routes to the school. Then the students would enter through a smaller side entrance in order to avoid the mob.

Reporters had also come to Daisy Bates's house to report the story. She asked the reporters not to follow the students for their safety. But she told four African-American reporters that if they were at the Sixteenth and Park Avenue entrance, they would see the Little Rock Nine enter the school.

The black reporters arrived at Sixteenth and Park streets before the students. As they got out of their car, the mob saw them and attacked. Shouts of "Get the niggers" echoed through the crowd. Two men lunged at the *Arkansas State Press*'s photographer, Earl Davy. They held him down and smashed his camera against the sidewalk. A burly man landed a blow to New York's *Amsterdam News* reporter Jimmy Hicks's shoulder. Hicks was spun around before he could run. He then hid between parked cars. Several other men hammered Alex Wilson, the editor of the *Tri-State Defender*. They knocked him to the ground and kicked his stomach. One hate-filled man raised a brick to smash Alex's skull. The reporters' lives were in grave danger. Then somebody yelled, "The niggers

An African-American reporter is attacked by the crowd outside Central High School.

are in the school!"[20] The mob rushed toward the police barricades that surrounded Central High.

During the brutal attack on the reporters, the students hurried out of the cars and entered through the side door. They were led through the unfamiliar halls. They tried to ignore the ugly words as chants of "the niggers are in" grew louder.

Inside Central High

The students met with Vice Principal Elizabeth P. Huckaby and received their schedules. The stress had been hard on Thelma Mothershed's heart. Her pulse was irregular and she was having trouble breathing. She sank to the floor and rested her head on a chair. Her lips and fingers were bluish. Huckaby called the school nurse to care for her. The other students were guided to their classes. None of the nine had any classes together. They would each have to face the white students alone.

Some white students left school once the black students arrived. Others made unfriendly remarks, spat at them, or attempted to move their chairs away from the black students. Some teachers were against integration, too. They allowed abusive remarks in their classrooms. But not all of the students or teachers were unfriendly. Huckaby was pleased to see one of her better students helping Jefferson Thomas understand an assignment. And Melba's shorthand teacher had complete control of her classroom. She tried to steer Melba away from the scene growing outside the window.

Melba looked out anyway. The mob had grown. It was a sea of angry faces pushing against the barricades. Chants of "Two, Four, Six, Eight—We ain't gonna integrate" could be heard through the school's brick walls.

The Mob Breaks Through

At around 11:30 A.M., Assistant Chief of Police Gene Smith realized his forces would not be able to hold the horde of people trying to get into the school. He ordered that the black students be removed from the school for their own safety. Teachers ran to gather the nine students. Melba recalls the look of fear on her guide's face as she was told to hurry to the principal's office and not stop for anything.

Assistant Chief Smith was determined to get the kids out of the school unharmed. He directed them to the basement. Outside the basement, two sedans waited with their engines running. The students were told to get in, lock their doors, keep their heads down, and hold their notebooks against the windows. Then Smith told the drivers to move fast and not stop.

The drivers gunned the engines and surged through the crowd. They accelerated as the mass of people parted. Terrence Roberts had no doubt that their lives were in jeopardy.[21] He could hear the voices yelling for their blood as they left the building. The cars were pelted with rocks as they made their escape.

Later, when everyone was safe, a reporter asked Daisy Bates if the students would return to Horace Mann, the all-black school. She said "No, they were going to remain out of the school until the president of the United States guaranteed them protection within Central High."[22]

Daisy Bates challenged President Eisenhower to rise to the occasion. But it was the mayor of Little Rock who sent an urgent telegram requesting help:

September 24, 1957, 10:37 A.M.

The immediate need for federal troops is urgent. The mob is much larger at 8 a.m. than at any time yesterday. People are converging on the scene from all directions. Mob is armed and engaging in fisticuffs and other acts of violence. Situation is out of control and police cannot disperse the mob. I am pleading to you as President of the United States, in the interest of humanity, law, and order, and because of democracy world wide, to provide the necessary federal troops within several hours. Action by you will restore peace and order and compliance with your proclamation.

Woodrow Wilson Mann,
Mayor of Little Rock, Arkansas[23]

The President Steps In

Midafternoon on September 24, President Dwight D. Eisenhower gave the order to send troops into Little Rock. That night, he addressed the nation from the White House. He spoke of the "serious situation" in Arkansas:

Disorderly mobs have deliberately prevented the carrying out of proper orders from a federal court. . . . I yesterday issued a proclamation calling upon the mob to disperse. This morning the mob again gathered in front of the Central High School of Little Rock, obviously for the purpose of again preventing the carrying out of the Court's order relating to the admission of Negro children to that school. . . .

> I have today issued an executive order directing
> the use of troops under federal authority to aid in the
> execution of federal law at Little Rock, Arkansas. . . .
> Mob rule cannot be allowed to override the decisions
> of our courts.[24]

The secretary of defense called more than one thousand paratroopers into Little Rock. The soldiers came from the 101st Airborne Division. They were military heroes known as the "Screaming Eagles." Army planes delivered the battle-equipped men to the city. A parade of jeeps and army vehicles carried them to Central High.

It was after midnight when the nine students heard that they would start school the next day. This time, they would go in with military protection. At 8:25 A.M. on September 25, 1957, the Little Rock Nine gathered again at Daisy Bates's home. Around fifty soldiers were waiting. Their boots and rifles shined. Battle helmets covered their heads. Some of the soldiers spoke into walkie-talkies. They told the Little Rock Nine that they would be riding to Central High in a jeep convoy.

Jeeps with gun mounts led and followed the army station wagon that held the students. A helicopter circled overhead. As they approached Central High, the students could see that the soldiers had blocked off streets around the school.

In the distance, the nine could still hear the chant "Two, Four, Six, Eight, We ain't gonna integrate."

A paratrooper stands guard on September 25, 1957, as Ernest Green (center) and Jefferson Thomas enter Central High School.

But the crowd was no longer a threat to the safety of the students or the school. The soldiers formed a box around the students and led them through the front doors.

The nine students were both proud and sad. When Minnijean Brown first saw the soldiers, she told Daisy Bates, "For the first time in my life, I feel like an American Citizen."[25] The others also were grateful that their country would go to such lengths so they could attend Central High. But as Ernest Green noted, "We got in, finally, because we were protected by paratroops." He was not sorry the president sent the troops. "[O]nly sorry it had to be that way."[26]

Even with the violence that occurred outside the school, the nine believed that the white students would like them if only they would get to know them. But most of the white students did not take the chance to find out.

The 101st Airborne Division is deployed to enforce integration at Central High.

CHAPTER *Five*

Surviving
Central High

For the most part, parents and students respected the law regardless of how they felt about desegregation. They hated the mob violence. Student editors wrote in the school newspaper, *The Tiger*:

> No matter what our personal opinions may be, we cannot be proud of the violence that occurred around our school that made it necessary for the use of these Federal troops. Looking back on this year will probably be with regret that integration could not have been accomplished peacefully, without incident, without publicity.[1]

An earlier student editorial had encouraged students to "meet the challenge" with maturity and intelligence. And another reminded students that less than one percent of the Little Rock population was in the crowd on September 23.[2]

In general, the students were concerned with their own affairs. Girls wore poodle skirts and bobby socks. The boys had crew cuts. They worried about their grades, after-school activities, and sports. They listened to music by Pat Boone, Elvis Presley, and Buddy Holly. They thought about things like the prom and dating. Most students chose to ignore the new African-American students.

But a group of segregationist students used every chance they had to make the nine African-American students' year a nightmare. These students yelled insults and threats, passed out mean-spirited flyers, spat on the African-American students, and even physically attacked them. The nine African-American students were often shoved, kicked, or tripped as they tried to attend classes.

White students who initially were friendly to these new students also received threats. Others, who may have wanted to become friends, were scared off by these actions.

Protection Is Minimal

The 101st Division had removed the crowd outside with efficiency and training. But inside the school they were told to stay in the background. Images of the armed guards entering Central High shocked the nation. False rumors that soldiers followed girls into the bathrooms spread and caused an uproar. School administrators wanting to regain control of

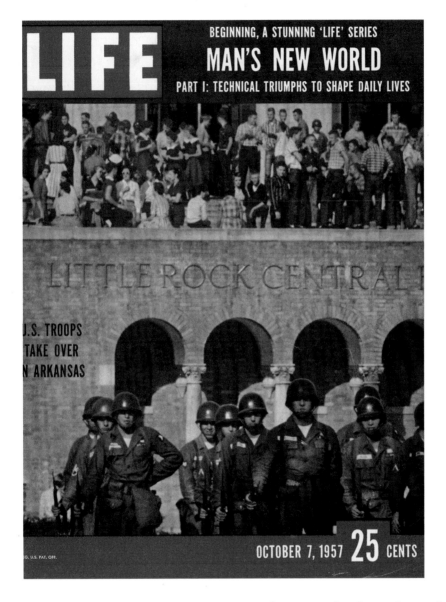

This cover of Life *magazine features a photograph of members of the 101st Airborne Division of the U.S. Army as they stand guard in order to enforce the desegregation of Central High School in October 1957.*

their school asked the guardsmen not to interfere. Furthermore, the soldiers were told not to enter classrooms, locker rooms, bathrooms, or assemblies. The school did not want the guardsmen to be a disruption.

The African-American students were often left to fend off their attackers themselves. Gym class could be especially hard. Terrence recalls one bully, Jerry Tuley, always lining up so that he could get in a quick kick or shove when the teacher was not looking. "[He] would place himself in the line behind me . . . if we did jumping jacks, [he] would kick forward instead of sideways; if we played basketball . . . I would be tripped or the ball would be 'passed' to me when I wasn't looking."[3]

Other attacks were more serious. In the locker room, a combination lock struck Terrence's temple and knocked him to his knees. He kept from falling by clinging to the locker's handle. If he fell, he was sure the attack would get worse. He stumbled into the coach's office. When he returned, the clothes in his locker were soaking wet. While he was with the coach, the boys had drenched his clothes.

Melba was walking down a hallway when a boy flashed a shiny object in her face. Suddenly there was intense pain and burning in her eyes. "I thought I'd die," she remembers. "I couldn't hear or see or feel anything except that throbbing searing fire centered in my eyes."[4] Some type of acid or alkaline had been sprayed on her. Droplets immediately faded her blouse. The soldier assigned to protect Melba helped flush out her eyes with water.

Elizabeth came into Vice Principal Huckaby's office during the second week of school. She had been crying. "I want to go home," she told Huckaby.[5] She was tired of the name-calling and being hit by objects thrown at her. She was sick of getting tripped and kicked; it was all too much. She did not even know her attackers.

Huckaby talked her out of leaving. She felt that if the black students backed down, the attacks would get worse and it would be harder for them to return. She also worried that it would make it more difficult for other black students to integrate. She appealed to Elizabeth's courage. Reluctantly, Elizabeth agreed to stay.

A Change of Guard

President Eisenhower calling on the Screaming Eagles to protect the black students was politically unpopular. Consequently, the president wanted to remove the troops from Central High School as quickly as possible. But the situation never became safe enough for him to remove the troops fully. However, in November, the 101st Division soldiers were replaced by members of the National Guard under federal orders. Some of these men were the same ones who had blocked the nine students'

Ernest Green shows his textbooks to young African-American children after his first full day at Little Rock Central High School.

entrance in September. These men were not as well trained as the 101st Division and there were fewer of them. Attacks on the nine students increased as their protection lessened.

Students regularly knocked the books out of Jefferson Thomas's arms. They kicked him as he bent to retrieve the books or sent his books flying down the halls. Once while he was standing at his locker, a boy landed such a brutal blow that Jefferson was knocked unconscious. His mother tried to keep him home the next day. But he told her, "No, if I stay out today, it'll be worse tomorrow."[6]

For all of the nine students, simply surviving at Central High was a daily battle. But as bad as it was, they did not always report the attacks to the teachers or principal. Reports not witnessed by a teacher would not be punished. Vice Principal Huckaby knew this was unfair. She also knew who the likely attackers were. But she believed suspending students based on unwitnessed accusations would cause more problems. It could give segregationists a way of removing the black students simply by lying. Huckaby felt that if white students were removed from school based on unwitnessed accusations from the black students, she would also have to remove the black students if the white students accused them of violent actions.[7]

How the Nine Coped

As the racial attacks continued, the nine students developed ways of handling some of the cutting remarks. They were inspired by civil rights leader Martin Luther King, Jr.'s actions. They read books by Mahatma Gandhi, who inspired King. Gandhi used nonviolent means to free India from British rule. King applied these nonviolent methods to the civil rights cause.

The nine students tried to follow the peaceful examples of these men. Melba said "thank you" to her attackers to show they could not get to her. Terrence invited boys who insulted his mother over to his house to meet her. As a group, the nine African-American students were determined not to give up. They leaned on each other as they tried to make it through the day.

The nine students received letters of support from people across the nation and around the world. Newspapers printed stories condemning the actions of Governor Faubus, the crowd outside the school, and others who were against integration. Several newspapers around the country ran a series of articles about the students such as "The Nine Who Dared."

Will Counts had photographed Elizabeth Eckford as she walked through the angry crowd the first day of school. His images gave the crisis a face—the face of a young dignified woman tormented simply because she was black. The picture was shown in newspapers across the country and made her a hero to many people outside her hometown.

Nonviolent Resistance

In the 1940s, Mohandas (Mahatma) Gandhi encouraged the Indian people to stand up to unfair laws but never to become violent. Although thousands of Indians were arrested, they continued to protest the laws of the British government that controlled India. Gandhi's movement received sympathy from around the world. The British did not know how to combat this nonviolent approach. Eventually, India gained independence from Britain.

Henry David Thoreau's essay "Civil Disobedience" and Gandhi's actions later influenced Martin Luther King, Jr. In 1955, King led the Montgomery bus boycott after Rosa Parks refused to give up her seat on a city bus. Large numbers of African Americans refused to ride the buses in Montgomery, Alabama, until the law forcing black individuals to sit in the back of the bus was repealed. It took a year, but the boycott succeeded and the buses were desegregated.

King continued to use nonviolent resistance in protests throughout the country. He and many others, black and white Americans, were arrested for their civil disobedience as they peacefully broke unjust laws and accepted the punishment.

The Little Rock Nine tried to help and support each other. Here some of them are pictured at Thanksgiving dinner in 1957 at the house of Daisy and L. C. Bates.

One day, a white stranger knocked on Elizabeth's door. He was carrying a watch and handed it to Elizabeth. It was from his wife. She was dying of cancer and wanted Elizabeth to have it.[8] Knowing they were valued elsewhere helped the Little Rock Nine make it through the year.

White Students Target Minnijean

The nine students came to Central High for its opportunities. Central High was five stories tall. It had well-equipped science labs; a greenhouse;

rooms and machines for vocational interests such as woodworking, plumbing, and drafting; and a library with eleven thousand books. It offered excellent college preparatory classes. Students put on fully-costumed plays in a two thousand-seat auditorium.

The nine students had been active in their old school. They were serious about their studies and enjoyed their extracurricular activities. Jefferson Thomas was a track star. Ernest Green played the saxophone. Melba Pattillo and Minnijean Brown loved to sing. But the black students had to give up their after-school activities if they wanted to attend Central High.

During his initial interviews with the black students, Superintendent Blossom told them that they would not be allowed to attend football or basketball games, participate in choir or drama club, or be on the track team. They could not go to prom or participate in other social events.[9] It was one of the ways the school board had reduced the number of students who wanted to integrate. It also was a way to maintain separation among the races. Segregationist parents worried that open social situations might lead to the black and white students dating— something that they were strongly against.

It was hard for the Little Rock Nine to give up the after-school activities they had enjoyed. But it seemed especially difficult for Minnijean. Minnijean had a fine voice and wanted to show the students at Central High that she had talent. She thought her ability to sing might help others accept her. She desperately wanted to fit in. Minnijean asked Vice Principal Huckaby if she could audition for the Christmas talent show. She had already been denied permission to sing at an earlier event. Huckaby said that the audition date had passed. Minnijean was heartbroken.

Minnijean's mother and Daisy Bates went to the school to discuss the situation. More importantly, they also wanted to discuss the lack of control the school had over the aggressive students. They talked about an episode in which Minnijean was kicked and nothing had been done about it. The principal said they had investigated, but since there were no witnesses, they were unable to verify the charge.[10]

Inaccurate reports about this meeting leaked to the press. The *Arkansas Democrat* printed that Bates and Mrs. Brown had come to Central High to protest Minnijean's not being in the talent show. This exposure made Minnijean more of a target for the segregationist students. Her expressive and reactive nature added fuel to the fiery situation. White students harassed Minnijean even more.

Just before winter break, the pressure got to Minnijean. It was lunch time. Minnijean had just filled her bowl with chili and was headed back to her table. Two boys pushed out their chairs to stop her from getting through. She was trapped. Other students kicked at her. The boys pulled their chairs back in. But as Minnijean started forward, they pushed them out again. This was not the first time things like this had happened in the lunchroom.

The cafeteria quieted as students noticed the conflict. Minnijean stood there, holding her tray above her head. She tried to get through, but could not. She wavered for a moment. Then she let go of the tray. As it crashed to the floor, hot, greasy chili splashed onto her tormentors.

Some of the black food servers clapped for Minnijean. They were tired of seeing the black students picked on. A teacher quickly escorted Minnijean and the two boys to the principal's office.

The boys claimed that moving their chairs had been an accident, but they also defended Minnijean. She was so often teased that they did not blame her for getting mad. They even suggested that she may have dropped the tray accidentally. The boys were told to go home and change. Minnijean was suspended for six days.

The principal warned Minnijean that another episode like the one in the lunchroom would lead to expulsion. To return, she would have to agree not to retaliate verbally or physically to any harassment.

The attacks against Minnijean increased when she came back. Her attackers wanted her to react.

They wanted her expelled. Once she was kicked so hard that she could not sit for two days.

On February 6, a girl following Minnijean kept stepping on her heels while chanting the word "nigger." As they neared the classroom, Minnijean had had enough. She swung around and called the girl "white trash." The white girl threw her purse at Minnijean and both girls were sent to the principal's office. The white girl went home, but Minnijean stayed at school. The principal thought it was best to wait before deciding on a punishment for the quarrel.

Students blamed Minnijean for the white girl going home and taunted her in the halls. During lunch, a boy poured hot soup down Minnijean's back. The boy routinely caused trouble and often harassed the African-American students. In the office, Vice Principal Huckaby asked him why he poured the soup on Minnijean. He said that he remembered "she had poured soup on some white boys and [so he] went over and dumped some on her."[11] The boy was suspended and Minnijean went home.

Shortly after, Minnijean learned she was expelled. The expulsion notice restated her agreement to not retaliate. Then it explained the reason she had been expelled: "After provocation of a girl student, [Minnijean] called the girl 'white trash,' after which the girl threw her purse at Minnijean."[12]

The real reason she was expelled had little to do with her name-calling. School administrators could not combat the growing hostility focused on Minnijean. She was a target, and it was easier to remove her than to deal with the aggressors. Huckaby was worried about Minnijean's safety and the safety of the other eight students if Minnijean remained at Central High. Huckaby wrote in her memoir that the expulsion of Minnijean was "an admission of defeat" on the school's part. "It was not volatile, natural Minnijean that was our difficulty. It was just that she and our impossible situation would not mix."[13]

Minnijean Brown smiles as she arrives at La Guardia Airport in New York after being expelled from Central High School in Little Rock.

The segregationists saw Minnijean's expulsion as a win. They had found a way to remove an African-American student from Central High. Signs were printed and students chanted, "one down and eight to go."

CHAPTER Six

Threats From Outside the School

Attacks did not come only from inside Central High. Segregationist groups that formed before the school year started continued their campaigns. Two pro-segregation groups, the Capital Citizens' Council and its sister organization the Mothers' League of Central High, were a constant aggravation and even a threat to the school. They claimed that they were against violence. However, many of its 514 members had been in the crowd outside Central High during the first days of integration. These groups held meetings, purchased ads, and encouraged the attacks inside the school. They harassed teachers and administrators and filed lawsuits to halt integration.

Early in the year, the Mothers' League tried to organize a student walkout. The walkout was scheduled for 9:00 A.M. The hall filled with a group of uncertain students. Teachers watched to see who would leave. Only about 150 students joined the protest. Half of those noticing the small numbers walked out the front door and came back in the side door. Suspensions were sent to about seventy students who had left the building.

Anonymous callers frequently claimed bombs were in the school. These calls were usually hoaxes. But occasionally the threat was real. Once dynamite was found in the school basement. Another time, firecrackers were found in a student's locker.[1] Real or not, these calls disrupted the school day and forced unplanned evacuations and costly searches.

Many of the threats targeted Daisy Bates and the nine students' homes and families. The school directory published all students' addresses and phone numbers, including those of the Little Rock Nine. This made it easy for segregationists to find out where the nine students lived. The students received hate mail. Their phones rang at all hours with abusive calls. Bomb threats were common. Once, someone called Terrence's mother to say her son had been seriously injured. She rushed to the school only to learn it was a prank.[2]

During the first year of integration, crosses were burned in the front yard of the Bates's home three times. The front-room picture windows were shattered so many times, that Daisy and L.C.

covered them with steel screens. Vandals set their house on fire twice. Their insurance company dropped their policy because of the number of claims. And the Bateses had to hire private guards to protect their home.

Protecting Private Records

In October, the Little Rock city council passed a law requiring organizations to give information about their members to any elected official who asked for them. The city council wanted to know who was supporting the NAACP. Daisy Bates refused to hand over the documents. She knew that giving the information would lead to harassment of NAACP members and donors.

Two weeks later, the city council ordered the arrests of NAACP officials because they refused to cooperate. Daisy Bates turned herself in to the police. The judge in Little Rock said the ordinance was valid. He fined Bates one hundred dollars plus legal costs. The NAACP appealed. The case went all the way to the U.S. Supreme Court. The Supreme Court declared the law unconstitutional and Bates did not have to pay the fine.

Daisy and L. C. Bates Lose Their Newspaper

Daisy Bates knew from the beginning that she was risking a lot by helping the black students integrate. Early in the fall, a white woman came to Bates and

The Little Rock Nine are escorted into Central High during the time that paratroopers were stationed there.

asked her to convince the black students not to attend Central High. Bates asked what would happen if she refused. The woman told her that her paper would fail. "You'll be destroyed," she said. "You, your newspaper, your reputation—everything."[3]

Daisy Bates did not back down. She would not abandon the nine students. During the crisis, advertisers pulled their ads from her newspaper. One longtime advertiser told Bates that he had been threatened. Someone had said his store would be bombed if he continued to support the *Arkansas State Press*. He was sorry, but he did not feel he could take the risk.

The Bateses tried to keep the paper running for as long as they could. Many letters of encouragement came into their office. A few letters contained cash gifts to help keep the paper going. But since papers do not charge a lot of money for each issue, they cannot survive without advertisers. Ultimately the segregationists won that battle. The *Arkansas State Press* went out of business.

Other Jobs Targeted

Some of the parents lost their jobs because they sent their children to the formerly all-white school. Threats to job security were some of the hardest to cope with. Without a paycheck, parents could not afford to feed their families.

The school where Melba's mother taught refused to renew her teaching contract unless she withdrew Melba from Central High. Melba recalls the food cupboards getting bare as her mother dealt with their financial crisis.[4] Melba's mother contacted the newspaper and the bishops in the area. With their help, she convinced the school to continue her employment in the fall.

CHAPTER Seven

Ernest Graduates

The NAACP asked for a formal hearing to challenge Minnijean's expulsion. The school refused to discuss the matter. Minnijean would not be allowed back at Central High. The New Lincoln School in New York gave Minnijean a scholarship so that she could attend school there. Psychologist Kenneth Clark offered her a place to stay. Before she left Arkansas, she told a reporter, "They throw rocks, they spill ink on your clothes, they call you 'nigger,' they just keep bothering you every five minutes."[1] Minnijean would finish her schooling away from the torments at Central High.

For the remaining eight students, the end of the year was getting closer and the attacks were getting worse. Their lockers were often broken into and their books and other items stolen. Melba said that the "barrage of flying food in the cafeteria got so bad that [they] could seldom eat [their] lunches there."[2]

Amid the turmoil, some students and teachers tried to help the African-American students. A boy named Link went to the segregationist meetings. Afterward, he called Melba and told her what they planned and places she should avoid.

Several teachers kept watch in the hallway between classes to help deter attacks. Gloria Ray was walking down the stairs when she heard a teacher scream out a warning. A boy was coming up from behind to push Gloria down the stairs. Gloria grabbed the railing and hurried down before the boy reached her. The teacher's warning saved Gloria from serious injury.

New Concerns for Ernest Green

The end of the year brought new concerns to Ernest Green's mind. He was the only senior in the group. The segregationists were looking for any reason they could find to exclude him from the graduation ceremony. Rumors were spreading that he would not be allowed to walk with the other Central High graduates. One student told Melba that for the African-American students it was not going to be a graduation; it would be a funeral.[3]

Ernest was under a lot of pressure. He wondered if they could stop him from graduating with his class. He wanted reassurance that he would be protected if he did. Daisy Bates met with Congressman Hays and visited the secretary of the Army at the Pentagon in Washington, D.C. Bates came back and told Ernest that there would be protection at the graduation.

There was also some concern about Ernest's grades. The physics teacher believed in segregation. He had not allowed Ernest to make up the work from the first three weeks of school when the African-American teens were barred from entering. Most of Ernest's grades were fine, but he needed to pass physics.

Ernest received a letter from an anonymous source. The letter asked that he not attend the graduation so that the white students could graduate without any trouble. Although the letter was signed "a worried senior," it was clearly written by an adult.

Ernest stayed home on the day of the senior picnic. But he did not intend to stay home for his graduation. He had gone through too much. He felt that graduating from Central [High] was bigger than just him. He figured if "one of us graduated, people could never refer to Central High as an all-white school again."[4]

Making Graduation Plans

The school began planning for the ceremony. Traditionally, students were called alphabetically— boy, girl, boy, girl. After receiving their diplomas, the boy and girl would walk down the steps together.

This was a problem. Although Ernest had never shown interest in any of the girls at Central High, the idea of a black and white couple was shocking in many places in America. In many states, it was illegal for a black person and a white person to marry. In some places, even the suggestion of a black man being involved with a white woman could lead to his murder.

The principal thought it would be best to let the girls know that they did not have to walk down the steps with Ernest. They could wait and leave a slight gap. Vice Principal Huckaby was uncertain exactly which girl would walk with Ernest. But she talked to the five girls whose names were near his alphabetically. One graduating senior, Ann Emerson, immediately said that she would have no problems walking with Ernest if her name was called.[5]

There were two graduation events at Central High. The first was an optional religious ceremony. It was scheduled the Sunday before graduation and took place in Central High's giant football stadium. The actual graduation was Tuesday. On that day, Ernest would receive his diploma. For both ceremonies, police and members of the National Guard would offer protection.

On Sunday, Ernest's parents arrived at the stadium early. At first, people seemed to be avoiding the seats around Mr. and Mrs. Green. But soon others arrived and sought out those seats as a sign

Ernest Green (left) became the first African American to graduate from Central High School.

of support. There were no incidents during the hour-long service. But afterward, off to the side, a senior boy spat on a young African-American girl who had been attending. Police arrested the boy.

On Monday, the seniors practiced for graduation. Before practice began, the class president, Ronnie Hubbard, spoke to the other seniors. "I know everyone will do what is right tomorrow night," he told them. "I don't think anyone wants to do anything to ruin our commencement." The seniors applauded, and practice went smoothly.[6]

A Surprise Visitor at Graduation

Tuesday was graduation day and tension permeated everything. Final exams had been graded and turned in. Ernest had passed all his classes and would walk on stage to receive his diploma. Captain Stumbaugh of the FBI assured Vice Principal Huckaby that the safety preparations were complete. He had even checked the upper windows of the houses over-looking the stadium for possible sniper positions.

In the stadium, the police presence was noticeable. The principal gave each senior only three tickets for family and friends. By doing this, he hoped to keep down the number of troublemakers.

At 8:00 P.M., six-hundred seniors in their caps and gowns proceeded into the stadium and found their seats. The program consisted of speeches and a long epic poem. There was no mention of the desegregation crisis.

Finally, the gym teacher began announcing the names of the graduating class. Ernest was Number 203. His name was called. He walked up the ramp and onto the stage. The principal handed him his diploma and then shook his hand. The few photo-graphers admitted to the ceremony tried to get the best pictures they could to send over the newswire. Ernest had made it. He was the first African

American to graduate from Central High.

On his way back from receiving his degree, Ernest was alone. The girl who had walked with Ernest at the religious service received so many negative phone calls that a teacher decided it was best if she left some space.

Watching Ernest receive his diploma and sitting with his parents was civil rights leader Dr. Martin Luther King, Jr. King had been speaking nearby in Pine Bluff, Arkansas, and decided to come see Ernest graduate. It did not matter what the rest of the crowd

Dr. Martin Luther King, Jr., who later delivered his "I Have a Dream" speech at the Lincoln Memorial in Washington, D.C., attended Ernest Green's graduation.

felt or that a few people had whistled while Ernest was on stage. He had graduated, and Martin Luther King, Jr., a hero in the civil rights movement, was there to see.

CHAPTER Eight

No School
for All

The school year was done, but the battle over integration was not. In June 1958, the school board asked the court for permission to halt integration until 1961. They based their argument on the chaotic year at Central High. Judge Lemley heard the case and granted the three-year delay. He said that while black students had the right to attend white schools, "the time ha[d] not come for them to enjoy [that right.]"[1] Melba worried that her year of torture had been for nothing.

The NAACP appealed to the U.S. Circuit Court of Appeals in St. Louis. The appeals court overturned the decision in August, but left time for the case to be heard by the U.S. Supreme Court. When Governor Faubus learned the delay was overturned, he called a special session of the legislature. A governor may call

Thurgood Marshall, center, sits with some of the Little Rock Nine on the steps of the Supreme Court building in Washington, D.C., on August 22, 1958. That day, he filed an appeal in the integration case of Central High School. Daisy Bates is to the left of him.

a special session to consider bills after the regular legislative session has finished. The bill that Governor Faubus wanted passed would give him the power to close all public schools to avoid integration. The state representatives voted overwhelmingly to pass the bill.

On September 12, 1958, three announcements were made that directly affected the African-American students at Central High. First, the U.S. Supreme Court ordered Little Rock to continue its planned integration. Within hours, the Little Rock school board announced that schools would begin in three days. These were the decisions the African-American students were hoping for.

Then on the very same day as those other two announcements, Governor Faubus used his new power and closed all the public high schools in Little Rock. Central High School; Hall High School, a segregated white school; and Horace Mann, the segregated black school, were closed by order of the governor. The citizens would vote in two weeks to decide if these schools should remain closed.

The Women's Emergency Committee

The citizens would vote in only a few weeks. One of the most respected senior citizens in Little Rock, Adolphine Fletcher Terry, organized a group of women to fight against the school closings. She called the

The Politics of Orval Faubus

It is surprising that an integration crisis happened in Little Rock, Arkansas. Little Rock was considered progressive before 1957, and Governor Orval Faubus initially seemed moderate on racial issues.

Faubus grew up in rural Arkansas. The son of a socialist, Faubus ran for office as a champion of the poor. Before the crisis, Faubus avoided taking sides on racial issues. He campaigned against an extreme segregationist and won. He appointed African Americans to state offices. After his election, two Arkansas school districts integrated without any major problems.

In 1957, Faubus faced a political crisis. A large number of voters were against integration. In order to be reelected, Faubus would have to side with the segregationists. His political ambition was stronger than any beliefs he held on racial equality. Calling out the troops to protect the nine African-American children would have placed him on the same side as the integrationists.

Faubus won four more elections after the crisis. He was the longest-serving governor in the state. But his name is forever tied to the crisis he helped create in Little Rock and the closing of the schools. By doing that, he sacrificed his state's reputation and his own ethics.

group the Women's Emergency Committee to Open Our Schools, or WEC for short.

WEC immediately began educating the public and working to get out the vote. But the vote did not come out in their favor. At the end of September, 19,470 people voted "against racial integration of all schools within the school district." Only 7,561 voted "for racial integration."[2] WEC was unhappy with the way the ballot was worded. The ballot did not ask about closing the schools. Instead it asked if the voter was for or against integration. The schools remained closed, but WEC did not give up.

Students Without Classrooms

Students in tenth through twelfth grade scrambled to find new schools. Some students were sent to live with relatives out of state. These students left their friends and families behind. It was hard, but in time most made new friends and found new opportunities.

Other students took long bus rides to schools outside the city. The additional students overcrowded the classrooms. Goforth Coleman hitchhiked almost twenty miles to school each way. "[T]he classes were so full—they had about 40 students per class," he recalled. "It was not a very conducive place for learning, yet the teachers worked real hard with us."[3]

Private schools opened for white students. At first, the school district tried to lease the closed schools to the Little Rock Private School

An unidentified African-American girl uses a television lesson to study at home after the schools were closed in Little Rock.

Corporation. The school district wanted to use public money to fund these segregated private schools. Judges at the Eighth Circuit Court of Appeals stopped this action. They said that the Supreme Court decision was the "law of the land" and the court would not allow "evasive schemes for segregation."[4]

Some schools opened inside churches. These schools had little time to hire teachers and plan for classes. Mary Peterson was starting tenth grade the year the schools were closed. Instead of attending Central High, she went to the school sponsored by the Second Baptist Church. The curriculum was basic, but she enjoyed eating lunch at a nearby drug store. She remembers an older teacher holding class on her porch when the teacher's arthritis acted up and another teacher sending students to her house to pick up things she had forgotten.

"Those were 'trustier' times," said Mary. She continued:

> I don't want to give the impression that the whole year was wasted. There were very good teachers there. . . . I remember capable teachers for world history and biology. I think part of the problem was having to hire people in a hurry and get a school up and running from the get go.[5]

The seven remaining African-American students were caught in the middle of this political tug of war. Melba remembers waiting. "I waited for legislators and Faubus and the NAACP to resolve the entanglement that surrounded Central High's integration. . . . I was alone, at home, waiting to restart my life— waiting to live my teenage years."[6]

For some students, the year was lost forever. As many as 45 percent of black seniors and 15 percent of white seniors in Little Rock did not continue their education that year.[7] Many of these students found jobs but did not graduate.

Although school was closed, extracurricular activities continued. There were dances, a school newspaper, and regular football games. But they were a poor substitute for school. Many football players were forced to decide which was more important: playing the game or getting an education by going to school out of the district. Football players lost their eligibility to play if they went to school outside the area.

When the season ended, the football players just left. Central High's team never even had a group photo taken. The other activities dwindled as parents realized the schools would remain closed.

Teachers Without Classes

The high school teachers' contract required them to be in the classroom from 8:30 A.M. until 3:30 P.M. every day. The teachers came, but there were no students. It was frustrating not to have students to teach. They began to teach each other. At Horace Mann, Principal Leroy M. Cristophe brought in lecturers from local colleges to teach his faculty. "Dr. Cristophe certainly kept us busy," remembered Jerome Muldrew, a young teacher at the time.[8]

The teachers were not allowed to teach outside of the schools until after 3:30 P.M. But many were committed to the education of children and would begin tutoring at 3:31 P.M.

In December 1958, the citizens elected a new Little Rock school board. The new board members were evenly split on the segregation issue. In May, the three board members who supported integration walked out of a meeting in protest. They were angry at what segregationists were proposing. They believed that the meeting would end after they left because there would no longer be a quorum. A quorum is the minimum number of people needed for voting to be allowed.

But the remaining members continued the meeting. Since a quorum was present when the meeting started, the decisions were still valid. The remaining board members fired forty-four teachers and school administrators who they believed favored integration. This included Vice Principal Huckaby, who the nine African-American students had turned to for help.

Huckaby and most of these teachers were beloved members of the community. They were fired because they had followed the law and tried to treat African-American children fairly. In response to these dismissals, city businessmen formed an organization called Stop This Outrageous Purge (STOP). They wanted the teachers rehired.

STOP joined WEC in an effort to recall the election of the school board members. They succeeded in forcing a new election. The vote was close. But the segregationists were voted out while the three moderate board members kept their positions. The new school board rehired thirty-nine of the forty-four teachers who had lost their jobs.

The Showdown Ends

The school closings lasted an entire academic year. Then in June 1959, the U.S. district court found the school-closing law unconstitutional. The school board chose not to appeal the decision.

Carlotta and Jefferson registered for Central High. They were the only members of the original nine still in high school. The NAACP had asked families to sponsor and give the remaining students places to live while they continued their education. Melba went to live with a family in Santa Anna, California. Terrence moved to Los Angeles. Thelma Mothershed took correspondence courses and earned enough credits to graduate.

With less than two weeks' notice, the school board announced that classes would start a month early on August 12. This surprise act limited the amount of time segregationists had to plan.

Even with late notice, around 250 protesters arrived at Central High on the first day of school. This time the police were ready and in control. They turned fire hoses on the members of the crowd who tried to break through the police lines. They arrested twenty-one people and the crowd scattered.

An African-American boy watches protesters heading from Little Rock city hall to Central High School in August 1959.

There were a few more incidents that year. Two women threw tear gas into the school during a school board meeting. There were no injuries. A dynamite blast wrecked an empty office at the school administration building. The planner of that attack had strong ties to the Capital Citizens' Council.

At the end of the school year, Jefferson and Carlotta joined Ernest as the first African Americans to graduate from Central High School. While the Little Rock schools would not be fully integrated until 1972, the crisis was over.

CHAPTER Nine

How Far We've Come

Forty years later, in 1997, the nine African-American students came back to Little Rock, Arkansas. Once again they stood before the entrance of Central High School. As before, a crowd of more than one thousand people gathered on the school lawn. But this time the people were not there to heckle or jeer.

This time, the crowd applauded and cheered as the nine were welcomed into Central High. The large cherrywood doors were held open for them by U.S. President Bill Clinton and the governor of Arkansas, Mike Huckabee.

Those who gathered came to mark the time as well as to forgive and be forgiven. They were there to both appreciate the progress that had been made and continue the work for a more unified country. President Clinton addressed the crowd:

> On September 4th, 1957, Elizabeth Eckford walked to this door for her first day of school, utterly alone. She was turned away by people who were afraid of change, instructed by ignorance, hating what they simply could not understand. And America saw her, haunted and taunted for the simple color of her skin, and in the image we caught a very disturbing glimpse of ourselves.
>
> We saw not one nation under God, indivisible, with liberty and justice for all, but two Americas, divided and unequal. . . .
>
> 40 years later, we know that we all benefit—all of us—when we learn together, work together, and come together. That is, after all, what it means to be an American.[1]

Over the years, the nine former students have come back to Little Rock for various occasions. The first time they all returned to Central High School was at the thirtieth anniversary of the crisis. When asked by a reporter what it felt like to be back, Melba Pattillo described it as "weird." Another member of the nine said it was "frightening."[2] That night, they talked as old friends with both laughter and tears as they remembered together.

Only one of the nine came back to live in Little Rock as a young person. Elizabeth Eckford returned to Arkansas at age thirty. She came back because she wanted to be near her family. She freely admits having post-traumatic stress disorder from her year

The Little Rock Nine pose on the lawn of Central High School in August 1997. From the left are: Carlotta Walls LaNier, Melba Pattillo Beals, Terrence Roberts, Gloria Ray Karlmark, Thelma Jean Mothershed Wair, Ernest Green, Elizabeth Ann Eckford, Minnijean Brown Trickey, and Jefferson A. Thomas.

at Central High, but she refuses to hate people. She was angry, but she has chosen to forgive.

A Second Chance at Friendship

In 1957, photographer Will Counts photographed Elizabeth Eckford walking in front of a hateful crowd. Her white and black skirt was starched and crisp. Dark sunglasses covered her eyes. Behind her was another young face. This girl's face was twisted with hatred and anger. The young white girl was Hazel Bryan. She was in the crowd yelling insults at Elizabeth. It is a photo that Elizabeth does not particularly like looking at.

The image was nominated for a Pulitzer Prize for photojournalism. The Pulitzer Prize is one of the highest American awards a person can win. The photo became a symbol of the civil rights movement. But pictures capture only a moment in time. Had things changed?

In this photo by Will Counts, Hazel Bryan (now Hazel Massery) screams slurs at Elizabeth Eckford as she tries to attend Central High School on September 4, 1957.

Forty years later, Will Counts was back in Arkansas covering the anniversary. He talked to Elizabeth Eckford and Hazel Bryan, now Hazel Massery, and asked if they would have their picture taken together forty years later.

In 1962, Massery had called and apologized to Eckford and to Eckford's grandmother. Hazel was only fifteen when the photo was taken. She was raised in a racist society and never questioned whether it was right or wrong. Massery says the birth of her first child opened her eyes. She became keenly aware of the pain she caused someone else's child. She looked at her heritage of hate and racism and decided not to pass it on to her children.[3]

"I was an immature 15-year-old," she said. "That's the way things were. I grew up in segregated society and I thought that was the way it was and that's the way it should be." Now she says she wants "to be the link between the past and the future. I don't want to pass this along to another generation."[4]

Both Eckford and Massery agreed to meet and be photographed. The two women talked as Will set up the photo shoot. The two mothers were older and more mature. As they talked, they found they had a lot in common. They decided to have lunch. Then they enrolled in a class on race relations together. The second photo ran on the front page of the *Arkansas Democrat-Gazette*. It was a symbol of healing and an acknowledgement of how far Americans have come.

Awards and Honors

After the black students' first year at Central High, the NAACP awarded Daisy Bates and the Little Rock Nine the Spingarn Medal. The Spingarn Medal is awarded annually for outstanding achievement by an African American. In 1999, the United States Congress awarded the United States Congressional Gold Medal to the Little Rock Nine. This is the highest honor the United States can give a civilian for service to the country. To many people the Little Rock Nine are heroes.

But they did not set out to be heroes. "We were not being courageous," explained Minnijean Brown, now Minnijean Brown Trickey. "We were kids who just wanted to go to school."[5] Elizabeth Eckford describes the nine as "ordinary people." But she reminds us all that "ordinary people can do extraordinary things."[6]

While the Little Rock Nine carry scars from their year at Central High, they would not change it. "I wouldn't take anything for our journey," said Ernest Green. "If one young person is inspired by the story, then the Little Rock Nine become the Little Rock 10, the 10 a hundred, the 10,000, the 10 million. . . ."[7]

The legacy of the desegregation of Central High School is much larger than the integration of a single school. The Little Rock crisis was a part of the American civil rights movement. The civil rights movement was the struggle of African Americans to gain the rights that were granted to all citizens by the Constitution. It was a chaotic time as people learned to give up their prejudices and embrace the ideas of equality.

In many ways, the civil rights movement started with the NAACP's effort to desegregate the schools and the *Brown* v. *Board of Education* decision. Those actions led African Americans such as Rosa Parks to stand up for their rights. Sit-ins and rallies followed. Martin Luther King, Jr., led two hundred thousand supporters to Washington, D.C. In 1964, all these efforts paid off. The United States Congress passed the Civil Rights Act and ended the Jim Crow laws.

The Civil Rights Act of 1964 grants equal access to public places such as restaurants, hotels, and movie theaters. And it entitles all people to the equal enjoyment of the goods, services, facilities, privileges, advantages, and accommodations of any place of public accommodation without discrimination by race, color, religion, gender, or national origin.

A Historic Site

In 1998, Central High School was named a historic site because of its importance in the civil rights movement. A well-preserved 1950s-era gas station across the street became a museum and visitor center. Elizabeth Eckford's daughter often guides people around the building. She works for the National Park Service. Inside are televised and printed images from the 1957 crisis. The Little Rock crisis was covered in depth by the media. Americans and world citizens alike were witnesses to the events. Their opinions, both horrified and shocked, may have helped President Eisenhower decide to call in federal troops.

In August 2005, the Little Rock Nine gathered again to unveil a statue in their honor. The sculpture by John and Kathy Deering shows the nine on their courageous walk to Central High. It is placed outside the governor's office where Faubus called out the National Guard to stand in their way.

In May 2006, Thelma Mothershed Wair and Elizabeth Eckford sank shovels into the dirt where a new visitor center would stand. The old visitor center was too small as the number of visitors continued to increase. The new building opened in September 2007 and is almost six times larger than the colorful little gas station. Much of the new center is devoted to telling the story of the 1957 desegregation. It houses materials related to the event and is a place where researchers can study those items. The new center also acts as a gateway for people who want to visit the historic neighborhood.

Perhaps the biggest tribute to what the Little Rock Nine achieved is the school itself. Central High School is fully integrated and educating students of all races together. "The bravery shown by these

Thelma Mothershed Wair, one of the Little Rock Nine who desegregated Central High School in 1957, helps break ground in May 2006 for the Central High School Visitor Center.

young people and their families changed the face of public education in this country," said Nancy Rousseau, principal of Central High School, talking about the Little Rock Nine. "Now, 2,400 students celebrate their differences every day, thanks to [their] courage."[8]

Moving Forward

Some of the Little Rock Nine speak at schools and colleges around the country. They do not want people to forget the importance of education and the dream of integration. But as President Clinton noted at the fortieth anniversary, while "segregation is no longer the law . . . too often, separation is still the rule."[9] The people of the United States are less racist, but the nation is still not fully integrated.

In school cafeterias, students of different ethnic backgrounds tend to eat together. Neighborhoods are often divided along ethnic lines. The public money spent on a student's education differs depending on where that student lives. Today's separation is not only by race but also by economic situation or the amount of money a family has.

The dream of a unified country is possible. But it will take the effort of everyone. The Little Rock Nine were teenagers when they broke the color line and stepped into Central High. Today, all students need to do is walk to a different table at lunch and meet someone new.

Civil rights activist Daisy Bates, in wheelchair, looks up at the Olympic flame she is carrying in Little Rock, Arkansas, on May 26, 1996. She was one of many torch bearers for the Olympic Games, held in Atlanta, Georgia, that year.

The Little Rock Nine gathered together again in September 2007 at Central High to celebrate the fiftieth anniversary of the school's integration. From the left are: Thelma Mothershed Wair, Minnijean Brown Trickey, Jefferson Thomas, Terrence Roberts, Carlotta Walls LaNier, Gloria Ray Karlmark, Ernest Green, Elizabeth Eckford, and Melba Pattillo Beals.

Standing outside Central High, President Clinton asked the young people to decide if they would be a "shining example or stunning rebuke to the world of tomorrow. . . . We are white and black, Asian and Hispanic, Christian and Jew and Muslim," President Clinton told the crowd. "But above all, we are still Americans. Martin Luther King said, 'We are woven into a seamless garment of destiny. We must be one America.'"[10]

The Little Rock Nine proved their potential during the crisis they endured as teenagers. They all went on to receive college degrees and have successful careers.

Melba Pattillo Beals

Melba Pattillo Beals received a bachelor's degree from San Francisco State University and a master's in communications from Columbia University. She has worked as a journalist for NBC and is the author of *Warriors Don't Cry: A Searing Memoir of the Battle to Integrate Little Rock's Central High.* A public speaker by nature, she often makes appearances to speak about the crisis.

Elizabeth Eckford

After completing her high school requirements, Elizabeth Eckford joined the U.S. Army. She attended Central State University in Wilberforce, Ohio, and returned to Little Rock in her thirties. Still shaken by her experiences, she avoided talking about the 1957 high school year until 1996. Now she talks with young people about the crisis as a way to promote healing. She is on the board of directors for the Central High Museum and Visitor Center and was recently working as a probation officer.

Ernest Green

Ernest Green received his master's degree in sociology from Michigan State University. He was the assistant Secretary of Housing and Urban Affairs during President Jimmy Carter's administration from 1977 to 1981. Green worked as Managing Director at Lehman Brothers in Washington, D.C., and served on the boards of the NAACP and the Winthrop Rockefeller Foundation.

Gloria Ray Karlmark

Gloria Ray Karlmark moved to Missouri and graduated from the Kansas City Central High School. She graduated with bachelor degrees in chemistry and mathematics from the Illinois Institute of Technology. Gloria has held jobs in countries around the world. She became a patent attorney in Sweden in 1977. She worked as a documentation specialist in Belgium and became the editor-in-chief for an international journal on computers in industry.

Carlotta Walls LaNier

Carlotta Walls LaNier graduated from Central High in 1960. She holds a bachelor of science degree from Colorado State. She worked with teenagers at the YMCA before founding a real estate brokerage firm.

Terrence Roberts

Terrence Roberts earned a bachelor's degree in sociology, a master's degree in social welfare, and a Ph.D. in psychology. He has worked in hospitals and was the department chair at Antioch University until starting a management-consulting firm. He continues to lecture about the Little Rock crisis around the country.

Jefferson Thomas

Jefferson Thomas graduated from Central High School in 1960. Drafted into the Army, he served his country again in Vietnam. He received his college degree from California State University in Los Angeles. He was an accountant for the United States Department of Defense and is now retired.

Minnijean Brown Trickey

Minnijean Brown Trickey graduated from New York's New Lincoln School in 1959. She attended Southern Illinois University, then moved to Canada where she received a master's of social work degree from Carleton University in Ontario and raised six children. She moved back to Arkansas in 2003. She is a social activist and lectures at colleges around the country.

Thelma Mothershed Wair

During the year without school, Thelma Mothershed Wair took correspondence courses and attended summer school. She received her Central High School diploma by mail. Thelma earned her master's degree in guidance and counseling from Southern Illinois University. She taught home economics for twenty-eight years before retiring in 1994.

Timeline

1954	May 17: The U.S. Supreme Court rules on the *Brown* v. *Board of Education* case, saying the doctrine of "separate but equal" has no place in public education.
	May 22: The Little Rock school board says it will comply with the Supreme Court ruling.
1957	August 27: A member of the Mothers' League of Central High School files a lawsuit asking a federal court to postpone the integration.
	August 30: Federal District Judge Ronald Davies rules that the integration must begin as planned.
	September 2: Governor Orval Faubus calls out the Arkansas National Guard to surround Little Rock Central High School and addresses the state.
	September 3: Judge Davies, believing that the Guard has been called to protect people and property, tells the NAACP to continue the planned integration.
	September 4: Elizabeth Eckford faces the angry mob alone and is stopped from entering the school by the National Guard; the other African-American students walking with ministers are also turned away.
	September 20: Judge Davies forbids Governor Faubus from further interference.
	September 23: The nine African-American students enter Central High through a side door; the angry mob attacks three African-American reporters; the nine students are removed from school for their protection.

September 24: President Eisenhower announces he is sending troops to carry out the court order.

September 25: The 101st Airborne Division escorts the nine African-American students into Central High.

December: After months of abuse by white students, Minnijean Brown drops food on two boys who are blocking her way; she is suspended for six days.

1958

February 6: After more harassment by white students, Minnijean is expelled from Central High for retaliating.

May 27: Ernest Green becomes the first African-American student to receive a diploma from Central High.

June 21: Federal District Judge Harry Lemley grants a three-year delay of integration that the school board has requested; the NAACP appeals.

August: Governor Faubus asks the state legislature to pass a law allowing him to close public schools to avoid integration; the legislature overwhelmingly passes the bill.

August 18: The Eighth Circuit Court of Appeals in St. Louis reverses Judge Lemley's ruling but grants the school board time for an appeal to the Supreme Court.

September 12: The Supreme Court rules that Little Rock must continue with its integration plan. The school board announces that school will begin in three days; Governor Faubus uses the new law and closes all of Little Rock's high schools.

September 27: Residents vote to keep the schools closed.

December 6: A new school board is elected; three members want to continue the integration; three members are segregationist and want to resist the court order.

1959 May 5: Those against segregation on the school board walk out of a meeting in protest; the three remaining segregationist members fire forty-four faculty who support integration.

May 25: Voters decide to remove the segregationist members from the school board; they also decide to keep the moderate members.

June 18: The school-closing law is ruled unconstitutional; school is scheduled for the following fall.

August 12: The school board opens public high schools a month early.

1972 Fall: All grades in Little Rock public schools are fully integrated.

1997 September 26: The fortieth anniversary of the integration of Central High School.

2006 May 20: Two members of the Little Rock Nine help break ground for a new museum and visitor's center.

2007 September 24: Celebrating the fiftieth anniversary of Central High's desegregation, the National Park Service formerly dedicates the new visitor center.

CHAPTER 1. **Facing the Crowd Alone**

1   Elizabeth Jacoway, *Turn Away Thy Son: Little Rock, The Crisis that Shocked the Nation* (New York: Free Press, 2007), p. 4.

2   Daisy Bates, *The Long Shadow of Little Rock* (Fayetteville, Ark.: University of Arkansas Press, 1986), p. 75.

3   Ibid., p. 70.

4   Ibid., p. 75.

5   Ibid., p. 70.

6   Melba Pattillo Beals, *Warriors Don't Cry* (New York: Washington Square Press, 1994), p. 50.

CHAPTER 2. **The Path to Equal Education**

1   Eric Foner, *Reconstruction*, ©1988. <http://www.njstatelib.org/NJ_Information/Digital_Collections/AAHCG/foner.html> (June 5, 2007).

2   National Historic Landmark Survey, "Racial Desegregation in Public Education in the United States Theme Study," *National Register, History and Education Program National Park Service Department of the Interior*, Washington D.C., 2000, p. 10.

3   Ibid., p. 12.

4   Roy Wilkins with Tom Mathews, *Standing Fast: The Autobiography of Roy Wilkins* (New York: De Capo Press, 1994), p. 234.

5   "Introduction to the Court Opinion on the *Plessy* v. *Ferguson* Case," Source 163 U.S. 537 (1896), *U.S. Department of State*, n.d., <http://usinfo.state.gov/usa/infousa/facts/democrac/33.htm> (December 2006).

6   Ibid.

7   National Historic Landmark Survey, p. 74.

8   Thurgood Marshall, *His Speeches, Writings, Arguments, Opinions, and Reminiscences*, ed. Mark V. Tushnet (Chicago: Lawrence Hill Books, 2001), p. 156.

9 | Howard Ball, *A Defiant Life: Thurgood Marshall and the Persistence of Racism in America* (New York: Crown Publishers), p. 17.

10 | Ibid., p. 123.

11 | "Introduction to the Court Opinion on the *Brown* v. *Board of Education* Case," Source 347 U.S. 483 (1954), *U.S. Department of State*, n.d., <http://usinfo.state.gov/usa/infousa/facts/democrac/36.htm> (December 2006).

CHAPTER 3. "The Nine Who Dared"

1 | Elizabeth Jacoway, *Turn Away Thy Son: Little Rock, The Crisis that Shocked the Nation* (New York: Free Press, 2007), p. 101.

2 | Ibid., p. 105.

3 | Daisy Bates, *The Long Shadow of Little Rock* (Fayetteville, Ark.: University of Arkansas Press, 1986), p. 133.

4 | Jacoway, p. 103.

5 | Melba Pattillo Beals, *Warriors Don't Cry* (New York: Washington Square Press, 1994), p. 40.

6 | Ibid., p. 38.

7 | Bates, p. 122.

8 | Ibid., p. 130.

9 | Ibid., p. 131.

CHAPTER 4. "The Need for Federal Troops Is Urgent"

1 | Daisy Bates, *The Long Shadow of Little Rock* (Fayetteville, Ark.: University of Arkansas Press, 1986), p. 4.

2 | Ibid., p. 8.

3 | Elizabeth Jacoway, *Turn Away Thy Son: Little Rock, The Crisis that Shocked the Nation* (New York: Free Press, 2007), p. 73.

4 | Bates, p. 57.

5 | Ibid.

6 | Ibid., p. 60.

7 | Ibid., p. 61.

8 | Benjamin Fine, "Militia Sent to Little Rock; School Integration Put Off," *Little Rock: 40 Years Later, New York Times Learning Network*, 1997, <http://www.nytimes.com/learning/general/specials/littlerock/090357ds-militia.html> (December 2006).

9 | Melba Pattillo Beals, *Warriors Don't Cry* (New York: Washington Square Press, 1994), p. 39.

10 | Ibid.

11 | Ibid.

12 | Bates, p. 61.

13 | Ibid., p. 63.

14 | Ibid., p. 64.

15 | Dwight D. Eisenhower, "Letter, DDE to Swede Hazlett, boyhood friend, Captain, USN, July 22, 1957," *The Eisenhower Presidential Center*, n.d., <http://www.eisenhower.archives.gov/dl/Civil_Rights_BrownvsBoE/DDEtoSwedeHazlett22July1957.pdf> (September 18, 2007).

16 | Dwight D. Eisenhower, "Diary notes DDE re mtg with Faubus," *The Eisenhower Presidential Center*, n.d., <http://www.eisenhower.archives.gov/dl/LittleRock/DiarynotesDDEremtgwithFaubus100857.pdf> (September 18, 2007).

17 | Ibid.

18 | Dwight D. Eisenhower, "DDE to Robinson june 4 58," *The Eisenhower Presidential Center*, n.d., <http://www.eisenhower.archives.gov/dl/LittleRock/DDEtoRobinsonjune458.pdf> (September 18, 2007).

19 | Beals, p. 93.

20 | Bates, p. 92.

21 | Terrence J. Roberts, "Fear Is Portable," *President Dwight D. Eisenhower and Civil Rights: Eyewitness Accounts*, 2000, p. 17, <http://www.eisenhowermemorial.org/DDEandCivil%20Rights-screen.pdf> (September 18, 2007).

22 | Bates, p. 93.

23 | Woodrow Wilson Mann, "Telegram Mann to President 9 24 57 pg1," and "Telegram Mann to President 9 24 57 pg2," *The Eisenhower Presidential Center*, n.d., <http://www.eisenhower.archives.gov/dl/LittleRock/TelegramManntoPresident92457pg1.pdf> and <http://www.eisenhower.archives.gov/dl/LittleRock/TelegramManntoPresident92457pg2.pdf> (September 18, 2007).

24 | "Dwight D. Eisenhower speech to nation September 24, 1957 transcript and audio," *American Radioworks*, n.d., <http://americanradioworks.publicradio.org/features/marshall/ike.html> (September 18, 2007).

25 | Bates, p. 104.

26 | Ibid., p. 106.

CHAPTER 5. Surviving Central High

1   Georgia Dortch and Jane Emery "The Price We Pay," *The Tiger: Little Rock Central High School Paper*, 1997, <http://www.centralhigh57.org/the_tiger.htm#Oct.%203> (September 18, 2007).

2   "Let's Keep the Record Straight," *The Tiger: Little Rock Central High School Paper*, 1997, <http://www.centralhigh57.org/the_tiger.htm#Oct.%203> (September 18, 2007).

3   Terrence J. Roberts, "Fear Is Portable," *President Dwight D. Eisenhower and Civil Rights: Eyewitness Accounts*, 2000, p. 18, <http://www.eisenhowermemorial.org/DDEandCivil%20 Rights-screen.pdf> (September 18, 2007).

4   Melba Pattillo Beals, *Warriors Don't Cry* (New York: Washington Square Press, 1994), p. 173.

5   Elizabeth Huckaby, *Crisis at Central High, Little Rock, 1957–1958* (Baton Rouge, La.: Louisiana State University Press, 1980), p. 52.

6   Daisy Bates, *The Long Shadow of Little Rock* (Fayetteville, Ark.: University of Arkansas Press, 1986), p. 126.

7   Huckaby, p. 85.

8   Elizabeth Jacoway, *Turn Away Thy Son: Little Rock, The Crisis that Shocked the Nation* (New York: Free Press, 2007), p. 194.

9   "Little Rock Central High School: The Little Rock Nine," *National Park Service, U.S. Department of the Interior*, n.d., <http://www.nps.gov/chsc/planyourvisit/upload/Site%20Bulletin%20Little%20Rock%20Nine.pdf> (September 18, 2007).

10   Huckaby, p. 93.

11   Ibid., p. 149.

12   Ibid., p. 152.

13   Ibid.

CHAPTER 6. Threats From Outside the School

1   Elizabeth Jacoway, *Turn Away Thy Son: Little Rock, The Crisis that Shocked the Nation* (New York: Free Press, 2007), p. 229.

2   Melba Pattillo Beals, *Warriors Don't Cry* (New York: Washington Square Press, 1994), p. 234.

3   Daisy Bates, *The Long Shadow of Little Rock* (Fayetteville, Ark.: University of Arkansas Press, 1986), p. 171.

4   Beals, p. 287.

Chapter Notes

CHAPTER 7. Ernest Graduates

1. Elizabeth Huckaby, *Crisis at Central High, Little Rock, 1957–1958* (Baton Rouge, La.: Louisiana State University Press, 1980), p.159.

2. Melba Pattillo Beals, *Warriors Don't Cry* (New York: Washington Square Press, 1994), p. 296.

3. Ibid.

4. Ernest Green, "Ernest Green Describes Experience at Central High," *Old State House Museum: The Arkansas News*, 2007, <http://www.oldstatehouse.com/educational_programs/classroom/arkansas_news/detail.asp?id=46&issue_id=5&page=4> (September 18, 2007).

5. Huckaby, p. 208.

6. Ibid., p. 210.

CHAPTER 8. No School for All

1. "Crisis Timeline," *National Park Service, U.S. Department of the Interior*, July 25, 2006, <http://www.nps.gov/chsc/historyculture/timeline.htm> (September 18, 2007).

2. Elizabeth Jacoway, *Understanding the Little Rock Crisis: An Exercise in Remembrance and Reconciliation*, eds., Elizabeth Jacoway and C. Fred Williams (Fayetteville, Ark.: University of Arkansas Press, 1999), p. 11.

3. Andrew A. Green, "Little Rock's 'Lost Class' of 1959 recalls turbulent year," *Arkansas Democrat-Gazette*, 1998, <http://www.ardemgaz.com/prev/central/acclass27.html> (September 18, 2007).

4. *Cooper et al.* v. *Aaron et al*, 358 U.S. 1958.

5. Mary Peterson, interview with author, August 2006.

6. Melba Pattillo Beals, *Warriors Don't Cry* (New York: Washington Square Press, 1994), p. 307.

7. Andrew A. Green, "Little Rock's 'Lost Class' of 1959 recalls turbulent year'" *Arkansas Democrat-Gazette*, 1998, <http://www.ardemgaz.com/prev/central/acclass27.html> (September 18, 2007).

8. Ibid.

CHAPTER 9. How Far We've Come

1 | Bill Clinton, "One America for today, tomorrow and forever, Clinton says," *Arkansas Online*, 1997, <http://www.ardemgaz.com/prev/central/prestext26.html> (September 18, 2007).

2 | Melba Pattillo Beals, *Warriors Don't Cry* (New York: Washington Square Press, 1994), pp. xx–xxi.

3 | Elizabeth Jacoway, *Understanding the Little Rock Crisis: An Exercise in Remembrance and Reconciliation*, eds., Elizabeth Jacoway and C. Fred Williams (Fayetteville, Ark.: University of Arkansas Press, 1999), pp. 20–21.

4 | Kevin Sack, "In Little Rock, Clinton Warns of Racial Split," *The New York Times*, September 26, 1997, p. A.1.

5 | P. J. Reilly, "'We Just Wanted To Go To School': Minnijean Brown-Trickey, One of the Little Rock Nine Still Fighting Racism," *Intelligencer Journal*, Lancaster, Pa., January 23, 2003, p.1.

6 | Kate Taylor, "Students Invite Real-Life Lesson in History," *The Oregonian*, Portland, Ore., March 17, 2004, p. C.01.

7 | Tulsa World, "Clinton Greets Famed Little Rock Nine / Today, Former Students Welcomed Among Cheers," *Tulsa World*, Tulsa, Okla., September 26, 1997, p. A.6.

8 | David Hammer, "Little Rock Statue Unveiled / New Monument Shows the Group in its Defiant Walk to First Day of School with Whites in '57," *Houston Chronicle*, Houston Tex., August 31, 2005, p. 03.

9 | Bill Clinton, "One America for today, tomorrow and forever, Clinton says," *Arkansas Online*, 1997, <http://www.ardemgaz.com/prev/central/prestext26.html> (September 18, 2007).

10 | Ibid.

accusation—A claim that someone has done something wrong.

appeal—To ask a higher court to review a lower court's decision.

barrage—A rapid attack or outpouring of something.

civil disobedience—Deliberate breaking of the law carried out as a nonviolent protest.

civil rights movement—Several years of nonviolent protests that ended racial segregation.

commencement—A graduation ceremony during which diplomas are given.

comprehensive—Covering many things so as to be complete.

conscience—An internal sense of what is right and wrong.

converge—To reach the same point from many directions.

desegregation—The ending of enforced separation of ethnic or racial groups.

discrimination—Unfair treatment of a person or group based on prejudice.

economic—Relating to money.

entanglement—A complicated situation.

ethnic—Relating to a group with distinctive cultural traits.

evasive—Intended to avoid something.

gradualist—Allowing change to take place slowly or gradually rather than suddenly.

injunction—A legal order that requires somebody to do or refrain from doing something.

integration—The process of opening a group, place, or organization to all people.

ordinance—A rule or law made by an authority such as a government.

permeate—To spread throughout so that every part is affected.

prejudice—An unfounded hatred, fear, or mistrust of a person or group, usually with regard to a particular religion, race, ethnicity, nationality, or social status.

progressive—Advocating social, economic, or political reform.

provocation—An act designed to make somebody angry or upset.

psychological—Relating to the mind and mental processes.

Pulitzer Prize—An annual award for excellence in American journalism, literature, and music.

purge—To get rid of opponents or people considered undesirable.

quorum—The minimum number of people needed for voting to be allowed.

scholarship—A sum of money awarded to help a student pay for education expenses.

segregation—Separation; often used to describe a practice of keeping ethnic, racial, or gender groups separate.

sit-ins—A form of protest in which people occupy a place and refuse to leave until their demands are met.

socialist—Someone who believes in a political system where the government owns the production of goods and distributes goods to the people.

thwart—To prevent somebody or somebody's plan from being successful.

turmoil—A state of great confusion, commotion, or disturbance.

unanimous—All members of a group are in agreement without dissent.

Further Reading

Books

Bolden, Tonya. *Tell All the Children Our Story: Memories and Mementos of Being Young and Black in America.* New York: Harry N. Abrams, 2001.

Fitzgerald, Stephanie. *The Little Rock Nine: Struggle for Integration.* Minneapolis: Compass Point Books, 2007.

Fradin, Judith Bloom and Dennis Brindell Fradin. *The Power of One: Daisy Bates and the Little Rock Nine.* New York: Clarion Books, 2004.

Mcwhorter, Diane. *A Dream of Freedom: The Civil Rights Movement from 1954 to 1968.* New York: Scholastic, 2004.

Polakow, Amy. *Daisy Bates: Civil Rights Crusader.* North Haven, Conn.: Linnet Books, 2003.

Price, Sean. *When Will I Get In?: Segregation and Civil Rights.* Chicago: Raintree, 2006.

Supples, Kevin. *Speaking Out: The Civil Rights Movement 1950–1964.* Washington, D.C.: National Geographic Society, 2006.

Internet Addresses

African American Odyssey—The Civil Rights Era
<http://memory.loc.gov/ammem/aaohtml/exhibit/aopart9.html>

Online News Hour—Remembering Little Rock
<http://www.pbs.org/newshour/bb/race_relations/july-dec97/rock_9-25a.html>

We Shall Overcome—Historic Places of the Civil Rights Movement
<http://www.cr.nps.gov/nr/travel/civilrights/ak1.htm>

Index

A

all-black schools, 24, 30, 31, 55
Arkansas Democrat, 72, 103
Arkansas State Press, 38, 40, 52, 80

B

Bates, Daisy, 38, 39, 40, 41, 43, 44–45, 48, 52, 55, 56, 57, 59, 72, 77–80, 83, 104
Bates, L.C., 38, 39, 40, 45, 77–78, 80
Blossom, Virgil, 30, 44, 71
Brown, Minnijean, 35, 59, 70, 71–75, 81, 104
Brownell, Herbert, 47
Brown v. *Board of Education*, 25, 30, 47, 50, 105
Bryan, Hazel, 102, 103

C

Capital Citizen's Council, 40, 76, 98
civil rights, 26, 39, 50, 68, 87, 102, 105
Civil Rights Act of 1964, 105
Civil War, 15, 17

Clark, Kenneth, 27, 81
Clinton, Bill, 99–100, 108, 110
Coleman, Goforth, 92
Counts, Will, 68, 101, 103
Cristophe, Leroy M., 95

D

Davies, Ronald N., 41, 44, 51
desegregation, 6, 30, 31, 33, 38, 44, 50, 86, 104, 106. *See also* integration.

E

Eckford, Birdie, 43
Eckford, Elizabeth, 8–9, 10, 12, 14, 33, 45, 47, 65, 68, 70, 100, 101–102, 103, 104, 106
Eisenhower, Dwight D., 29, 47–48, 50, 56, 65, 106

F

Faubus, Orval, 14, 40–43, 47–48, 51, 68, 88, 90–91, 94, 106
Fifteenth Amendment, 16, 17, 18
Forten, Charlotte, 16
Forten, James, 16

Index

Fourteenth Amendment, 15, 17, 18, 19
Freedman's Bureau, 16

G

Gandhi, Mahatma, 68, 69
Green, Ernest, 33, 59, 71, 82–85, 86–87, 98, 104
Griffin, Marvin, 40

H

Hall High School, 90
Hamilton, Charles, 23
Harlan, John Marshall, 19
Hicks, Jimmy, 52
Horace Mann, 55, 90, 95
Howard University, 23, 24
Huckabee, Mike, 99
Huckaby, Elizabeth P., 54, 65, 67, 72, 74, 75, 84, 86, 96
Huston, Charles, 23–24

I

integration, 25, 30, 31, 34, 40–41, 44, 51, 54, 57, 61, 65, 68, 71, 76, 77, 78, 88, 90–92, 94, 96, 98, 104, 108. *See also* desegregation.

J

Jim Crow laws, 17–18, 105

K

King, Martin Luther, Jr., 68, 69, 87, 105, 110
Ku Klux Klan (KKK), 6

L

Little Rock Private School, 92–93
Lorch, Grace, 10, 12, 47

M

Mann, Woodrow Wilson, 51, 56
Marshall, Thurgood, 24–25, 26, 27, 29, 30, 48, 51
Mothershed, Thelma, 35, 54, 97, 106
Mothers' League of Central High, 76–77
Murray, Donald, 24

N

National Association for the Advancement of Colored People (NAACP), 22, 23, 24, 25, 26, 30, 38, 39, 40, 44, 78, 81, 88, 94, 97, 104, 105
National Guard, 8, 41, 51–52, 65, 84, 106
New Lincoln School, 81

O

101st Airborne Division, 57, 62, 65, 67

P

Parks, Rosa, 37, 69, 105
Pattillo, Melba, 12–13, 20, 33–35, 42–43, 47, 51, 54–55, 64–65, 68, 71, 80, 81–82, 88, 94, 97, 100
Peterson, Mary, 94
Plessy v. *Ferguson*, 18–19, 21–22, 29
Potts, Marvin, 51

R

Ray, Gloria, 36, 82
Reed, Murray O., 40–41
Roberts, Terrence, 37, 55, 64, 68, 77, 97
Robinson, Jackie, 50

S

Second Baptist Church, 94
segregation, 5, 19, 24, 25, 29, 40, 42, 44, 48, 62, 67, 72, 75, 76, 77, 80, 82, 83, 91, 93, 96, 97, 108
slavery, 6, 15–18
Smith, Gene, 55

Spingarn medal, 104
Stop This Outrageous Purge (STOP), 96

T

The Tiger, 61
Terry, Adolphine, Fletcher, 90
Thirteenth Amendment, 15
Thomas, Jefferson, 35, 41, 54, 67, 71, 97, 98
Thoreau, Henry David, 69
Truman, Harry S., 22

U

U.S. Supreme Court, 5, 6, 19, 21, 22, 25, 26, 29, 47, 48, 50, 78, 88, 90, 93

W

Walls, Carlotta, 37, 97, 98
Warren, Earl, 29
Wilson, Alex, 52
Women's Emergency Committee to Open Our Schools (WEC), 92, 96
World War II, 21–22, 33, 38